PRAISE FOR
EXPANSIVE IMPACT

"You know that feeling when, try as you might, you just can't change the people and systems that are inhibiting you as a leader? Do you yearn to create impact and meaning, and yet external reality presents a stubborn blockage?

This book is your antidote. The Six Invitations of Expansive Impact empower you to harness what's inside you to create expansive impact around you. Rather than leading with exhausting brute force, Sarah lights the way to leading with ever-replenishing interior force.

Along the way, Sarah's wise, warm, and crystal-clear storytelling makes this read not only provocative and powerful but inspiring and uplifting. It would be impossible not to expand your impact after reading this book."

—LINDSAY PEDERSEN, Brand Strategist and author of *Forging an Ironclad Brand*

Exquisite. *Expansive Impact* is the modern-day leadership playbook for conscious business. With warmth and wisdom, Sarah offers powerful insights and self-inquiry for new and seasoned managers alike. Turn to any page for thought-provoking questions and team-building prompts, and buy a copy for everyone on your team to inspire a powerful new phase of their leadership journey. May we all 'look through the mirror, not the window' as we work to create the change so desperately needed in the world."

—JENNY BLAKE, author of *Pivot* and *Free Time: Lose the Busywork, Love Your Business*

.

Today's leaders are navigating complex global circumstances more than ever before. Our desire to have an impact on systems change and the world around us is growing. *Expansive Impact* is a reminder, a guide, and a practice for how to stay in relationship with ourselves, others, and the ever-changing world around us. Sarah invites us all to start choosing discernment over judgment, patience over pressure, and love over fear as a new way for leaders to uphold their strategy and leave their legacy."

—CAREY BAKER, CPCC, Co-CEO of the Co-Active Training Institute

Leading meaningful change in today's world can be incredibly challenging. Sarah's work provides a framework and path for those of us looking to achieve incredible results while leading from our heart. I'm forever grateful for the work Sarah has pioneered—it has fundamentally shifted how I show up and lead."

—LUKE BONNEY, Co-Founder and CEO of Redox

An utter delight. *Expansive Impact* is *the* guide to leading with intention and impact. Packed with insights and written with grace and clarity, this book offers thought-provoking observations, advice, and practical solutions to everyday leadership challenges. It provides creative ideas and self-reflective inquiries to put into practice with ease, and teaches you how to show up consciously as the leader you want to be in everyday moments."

—DR. HELEN KRUG VON NIDDA, Executive Coach and Founder of With Helen

Expansive Impact is just that—expansive! If you're tired of forceful and one-size-fits-all leadership approaches, look no further. Sarah Young will take your hand and guide you through a process that will allow you to discover not only who you are and what you stand for, but also create and step into a leadership vision for yourself that is cloaked in depth and compassion. *Expansive Impact* is a salve to the leadership wounds of today. Sarah Young will help you become the thoughtful and expansive leader so many of us are deeply craving to be."

—LAURA GARNETT, author of *The Genius Habit* and *Find Your Zone of Genius*

www.amplifypublishing.com

Expansive Impact: An Invitation to Lead in Everyday Moments

If you are interested in purchasing copies of this book for your team or organization or making a bulk purchase, please visit zingcollaborative.com.

The publisher and the author assume no responsibility for errors, inaccuracies, omissions, or any other inconsistencies herein. All such instances are unintentional and the author's own. The advice and strategies found within may not be suitable for every situation.

Throughout this book, some names and identifying characteristics have been changed or combined to protect the privacy of featured individuals, organizations, and situations and to uphold strict standards of confidentiality.

For more information, please contact:
Amplify Publishing, an imprint of Mascot Books
620 Herndon Parkway, Suite 320
Herndon, VA 20170
info@amplifypublishing.com

Library of Congress Control Number: 2021924428
CPSIA Code: PRFRE0122A
ISBN-13: 978-1-64543-971-4

Printed in Canada

For My Clients,
Thank you for the honor and privilege of
walking alongside you on your journey.

AN INVITATION TO LEAD
IN EVERYDAY MOMENTS

EXPANSIVE
IMPACT

SARAH YOUNG

CEO, ZING COLLABORATIVE

CONTENTS

BE CURIOUS: LEAD BY LISTENING FOR CLUES

BE COURAGEOUS: LEAD WITH TRUTH FROM THE HEART

BE CREATIVE: LEAD WITH AGILITY

CONCLUSION AND REFLECTIONS

INTRODUCTION

STANDING IN A
SPIRITUAL TORNADO

*She stood in the storm, and when the wind did not
blow her away, she adjusted her sails.*
—Elizabeth Edwards

t is 4:00 p.m. on a Thursday, and Cecilia just wrapped up an all-team meeting. During the meeting, she was charged with communicating her company's new remote-work policy. It is a policy that she doesn't entirely agree with, and that she wasn't able to successfully influence from within her role as the VP of communication.

Earlier in the day, Denise, a rock star on Cecilia's team who is leading a project for the company's highest-profile client, resigned. Denise said that she was ready for a change and was going to take three months off before joining a new start-up in an adjacent industry.

Cecilia alternates between gazing out the window and reviewing the leadership feedback surveys that she recently received from her team. A third of her team members shared that they find her style to be too hands on, and at times they feel like she micromanages. Another third shared that her style is too hands off, and that they desire a greater level of support and coaching. The remaining feedback was scattered across the board.

As the clock moves toward 4:45 p.m., she realizes that she is already running late for a walking meet-up with a friend across town. The Thursday walking meet-ups are an attempt to create more balance throughout the week.

Just then, the phone rings. The quality lead on the West Coast just discovered a significant issue in one of the distribution centers. Mislabeled products have been shipping for the last two weeks, and Cecilia now needs to figure out how to message this to clients. She texts her friend to let her know that she'll have to skip this week's walk (again).

While Cecilia believes in the work of the organization and feels a great sense of love and commitment toward her team, she is struck by a sudden feeling of defeat. It feels like the further she has advanced as a leader, the harder it is to feel successful. She has few colleagues at work who she can openly talk with about these challenges, as many of her former peers are now her direct reports.

On top of all of this, she feels a slight fracture within herself, as though there is a version who shows up at work each day as a manager and a leader and then a version who shows up in the rest of her life. The non-work version of Cecilia feels so much *freer.* The non-work version of Cecilia feels untethered to the projects, issues, and changing priorities that fill her workdays to the brim. Today alone she was on the phone for seven hours straight. This free and untethered self seems to be making fewer and fewer appearances lately.

Cecilia notices a feeling of loneliness within her body, alongside a desire for more ease and joy throughout the week. She momentarily daydreams about the early days, before having this level of responsibility, when the quality issue would have been someone else's problem to solve. She wonders: Is it possible to ever feel entirely successful as a leader? Or is leadership just a constant game of Whac-a-Mole, batting down one problem that pops up, only to find a new one emerging?

She snaps herself back to the moment, opens her laptop, and dives into the quality issue with the distribution center. She breaks her self-imposed "no coffee after 4:00 p.m." rule by topping off her cup with dark roast. She grabs a snack from the kitchen; it looks like it will be a long night.

Have you ever experienced a fracture within yourself, between the part of you who goes to work and the part of you who shows up in other areas of life? Perhaps it was a fracture based on values, where you were forced to choose between what you felt was right and what you were asked to do. Or maybe you have experienced a lonely leadership moment, in which you found yourself looking around and then looking within, unsure what to do next.

One of my earliest lonely leadership moments came toward the beginning of my professional career. I was working for a technology company, and my first trip with the company involved supporting a healthcare organization out East. Arriving on site the first day, my world expanded instantly as I observed individuals with gunshot wounds wearing shackles, saw visible bullet holes through patients' backs, and met a nude woman in the restroom who was bathing herself in the sink.

Returning to my hotel room each evening after my shift, I remained awake for nearly the entire night, unable to sleep as the events of the day replayed themselves in my mind. While we had been trained prior to the trip on how to use the software, we certainly hadn't been trained for this. My head was spinning, and I didn't know how to process what I was seeing each day. I slept only a few hours in total over the course of the seven-day trip, attempting to reconcile the work I was there to do, which involved software, with the amount of pain and suffering that was present, which involved people.

Another lonely leadership moment came several years later, when I was working on a team of people responsible for making some of the hardest decisions of my entire career. I will never forget the call that I received one day while I was working with a client in the Southwest. I was passing by the outdoor hotel pool on the way back to my room, when the phone rang. "Sarah," my colleague Larry asked, "should this person be let go?"

The person in question was not my direct report, but rather the direct report of a manager who had not provided any feedback for the entirety of his team member's career. In that moment, a passion burned within me to set the same expectations for our managers and leaders as we do for our direct reports. It felt both tragic and unfair that careers and lives were being uprooted and upended due largely to poor management and ineffective leadership. Once again, I grappled with a tension between the events of the projects and the impacts to the people on the projects.

This moment lit a spark of inspiration within me to empower and support leaders to effectively coach, manage, and communicate with those they're leading. I wanted managers and leaders to feel—and to *be*—successful and impactful in their roles. I wanted to avoid future instances of the scenario that I found myself navigating with Larry via phone on that warm, sunny day in the Southwest. I wanted to improve the statistic in which less than 30 percent of managers strongly agree that someone at work encourages their development.[1]

This spark of inspiration would eventually become my business, Zing Collaborative, which is focused on precisely that. Zing Collaborative is focused on coaching, developing, and partnering with individuals, teams, and organizations that want to increase their impact in a way that feels joyful, expansive, and alive. Today, I'm grateful to work with leaders who want to grow, evolve, and expand—both for themselves and for the benefit of their teams, organizations, and societies. This work takes many forms, including:

- Nature-based leadership experiences
- Virtual and in-house leadership programs for managers, leaders, and teams
- Consciously designed coaching circles and gatherings for high-impact, heart-centered humans
- 1:1 and small group leadership, CEO, and executive coaching

Zing Collaborative is also a member of 1% for the Planet,[2] which means that 1 percent of all sales is donated to approved nonprofit organizations working to protect our planet.

Creating Expansive Impact invites us to show up, stretch into, and explore all of the dimensions of who we are, in service of creating positive ripples in our leadership and our lives. Expansive Impact is based on the idea that leadership starts within and that we continuously have a choice about how we respond to our external circumstances and how we engage with the world and people around us.

No matter which form it takes, creating Expansive Impact can be joyful and fulfilling, but it is not for the faint of heart. It tests our integrity, our resilience, our character, and our capacity. It may call us forth and push us to our limits. It may also force us to face, and then reckon with, uncomfortable truths about ourselves.

The fact that you are holding this book in your hands means that you are part of the change toward a more conscious and compassionate world—a world where we can honor both people and projects, a world where who we are and how we lead can coexist harmoniously, and a world in which conscious leadership paves the way toward a better future for us all.

My most significant leadership lessons have not come from the recognition and rewards or from isolated moments on the highlight reel. Rather, they have come from the moments of the mess, the hardship, and the pain. In my work, they have come in the moments when I've been forced to look in the mirror and ask, "Is this the type of leader who I want to be?" and "What on earth am I supposed to do, when I have no idea what to do?"

In my personal life, the greatest lessons have come in the difficult moments that you have likely experienced in some form as well: if, for example, you have lost a loved one; experienced a chronic illness or significant challenge; navigated any sort of addiction or loved someone who has; grappled with a mental, emotional, or spiritual imbalance of any sort; or found yourself in what my friend Susan beautifully describes as a spiritual tornado. More than any book I have read or any program I have completed or any award I have won, my greatest growth has come in *these* moments—the moments when I'm forced to look within, over and over again, from the depths of anger, hurt, grief, confusion, or despair.

I share this peek behind the curtain because I believe that it is important for me, as your guide throughout this book, to acknowledge that my own path has been messy and imperfect. I have navigated situations where my leadership-related tools didn't work. There are others that I would go back in time and approach much differently if I could. In these situations, when it seems like we have exhausted the options in our toolbox and we are facing darkness and confusion, our opportunity is to continue to look inward, to do our deep work, and then to keep going.

THE SIX INVITATIONS OF
EXPANSIVE IMPACT

C reating Expansive Impact is a way to generate ongoing positive change within our lives—spanning both the personal and professional—without relying on outside circumstances and without requiring anyone else to change their behavior. That's right—it is a way to create the change we desire *without* forcing other people to change.

It is a way to create profound shifts through a combination of *how* we show up (our mindset and perspective) and *what* we do (our actions, behaviors, and approach). It invites us to first focus on the things that we can control, and then to notice the ripples of impact that we create as a result. This book is meant to be an almanac for your messy leadership moments—a guidebook of sorts, for your own leadership journey.

Throughout this book, we will hold the idea of both/and—both leading with our full and imperfect humanity, and honoring the very real demands of our leadership, our lives, and our everyday reality. This means accepting the sometimes-competing expectations of being a human and a leader; being someone who is accountable for core job responsibilities while also leading, managing, and coaching others; being someone who needs to get things done under urgent timelines, while also stepping back to think strategically and see the big picture. My wish for you, throughout the pages ahead, is twofold:

- First, to take a journey of self-discovery during which you will learn more about who you are as an individual and a leader and how to apply these findings back out in the real world.
- Second, to provide you with tangible, concrete tools, ideas, and examples that you can integrate into your own leadership—tools that you can refer to and rely upon when you're facing tricky situations or navigating spiraling thoughts.

Through conscious, intentional, and expansive leadership, we can together create a more conscious, intentional, and expansive world—a world in which we take time to recognize and appreciate each other as individuals, a world in which we're willing to become and remain curious, and a world in which we're willing to look within ourselves to discover how we are complicit in creating some of the things that we don't desire. Together, and throughout this book, we will explore leadership...

- Not only as something we do, but also as an expression of who we are.
- Not only as something we practice at work, but also something that we practice and implement in all dimensions of our lives.
- Not as an opportunity to create followers, but as an opportunity to take a stand for something bigger.
- Not as a way of promotion, but rather of attraction.
- Not as a form of persuasion, but of conscious positive impact and influence.
- Not as something that comes with a role or a title but that lies intrinsically within each of us.
- Not as something that happens only in large, sweeping initiatives but also in everyday moments.
- Not as grinding, driving, or forcing, but as pausing, slowing,

reflecting, observing, and creating from whatever is happening in front of, and within, us.

- Not as a rigid set of rules to follow, but as something that is creative, dynamic, evolving, and continuously being shaped and reshaped by that which is happening around us.
- Not as a mold or a set of predetermined characteristics to fit into, but as something that we can practice authentically, as the full expression of our higher selves.
- Not as something we do only with our team members, but also with the parking garage attendant, the server at our favorite restaurant, and the customer service representative on the other end of the phone.

This is not a how-to book on leadership. This is not a book that offers up a formulaic list of ten quick steps to be a great leader. The world, and our collective bookshelves, have plenty of those. This book is meant to be a guided inner journey. It is an opportunity for you to pause, step back, and consider who you are and who you want to be, both as a leader and a human being. It is a reflective experience that invites us to do the brave and vulnerable work of looking in the mirror at who we are, how we are showing up, and what is getting in the way of creating the type of impact that we desire with our teams, our organizations, our businesses, our families, our friends, and our world.

Out beyond ideas of wrongdoing and rightdoing,
there is a field. I'll meet you there.
—Rumi

We will work together to create Expansive Impact via six invitations, which we will examine together on the pages that follow.

The Six Invitations of Expansive Impact

1. BE COMPASSIONATE: Lead with Love.

2. BE CONSCIOUS: Lead from Within.

3. BE CLEAR: Lead in Relationship to Reality.

4. BE CURIOUS: Lead by Listening for Clues.

5. BE COURAGEOUS: Lead with Truth from the Heart.

6. BE CREATIVE: Lead with Agility.

We will journey together through these six invitations. Along the way, we will hear from thought leaders and researchers, and from plenty of people like you and me who have wondered...

Now What?

What do we do when we don't know what to do, when we've tried out all of the tools we have, or when we're facing our very own spiritual tornado of leadership?

How do we handle the hard and uncomfortable moments, the difficult conversations, the existential questions that inevitably arise when we decide to show up and lead?

What do we do when we are faced with the choice to stay true to ourselves and our values or to do what is being asked of us in the given moment?

In a recent leadership experience, Shay, a smart, thoughtful, kind, and detail-oriented project manager, said, "I just want to go into the leadership factory—and come out a different person, a better leader."

Here's the good news. We don't have to go into a leadership factory, and we don't have to become different people. Rather, we can become more expansive versions of ourselves by exploring, and then stretching into, the various dimensions of who we already are. This doesn't mean that we gloss over areas where we can grow and improve, but it means that we are focused first and foremost on stretching into the fullest, most expansive, and most authentic version of who we are. By doing this, we grow our capacity to navigate even the toughest situations and the fiercest of spiritual tornados. From here, we can create our unique leadership footprint on the world, by leading from our own inner truth and power.

One of my own spiritual tornados of leadership came when I received a piece of feedback that I'll never forget.

BE COMPASSIONATE:

LEAD WITH LOVE

THE ANTI-MARSHMALLOW CAMPAIGN

A true hero is an ordinary person who can hold the sword of truth and tell the full truth of herself, in her good, her bad, and her ugly qualities. She makes her choices from this understanding. As heroes, we move forward, not in fear and anger, but in integrity, love, and vision. We work from the strength of our spines rather than the breathlessness of our chests.

—Zainab Salbi, *Freedom Is an Inside Job*

still have the purple notebook that I was using at the time. Written across the top, circled, and underlined are the words "Anti-Marshmallow Campaign."

"Sarah, you're too compassionate. Like a marshmallow. We need to put you on the Anti-Marshmallow Campaign."

I had just received this feedback in a meeting with my leader. I diligently wrote down every word, nodding and taking it to heart. I was committed to taking the feedback seriously, to improving in this area, to embarking on the Anti-Marshmallow Campaign. The bottom line of the feedback was this: to successfully do this job, in this leadership role, your compassionate approach is not cutting it.

In the weeks that followed, I launched my Anti-Marshmallow Campaign in earnest. I revisited my purple notebook daily, reflecting on the words *Anti-Marshmallow Campaign* and considering how, on that particular day, I could improve my leadership abilities by being less compassionate. I practiced this for several weeks, attempting to be more results focused, less people focused, and less *soft*.

I continued to engage with this personal leadership initiative, feeling a numbness inside me that was increasing by the day. I was so focused on taking this feedback to heart that I found myself making entirely avoidable and even embarrassing mistakes. My focus on being less compassionate was taking a tremendous amount of energy, as it was misaligned with my natural way of being. It is exhausting to force ourselves to be something that we naturally aren't.

After a few weeks of the campaign and noticing these feelings of numbness and exhaustion within myself, I had a profound realization: to be less compassionate, for me, anyway, is to silence a core part of myself. I have always been compassionate. It is part of who I am. To become less compassionate is to become something I'm not—it throws me out of alignment and takes me away from my core, true self. To be compassionate is to be like water. It can be soft, gentle, and flowing. And, water can be the strongest force. Additionally, I realized that living in alignment with our values, rather than numbing out to get the job done, is what takes true strength. When we, over time, kill off parts of ourselves to chase external success or outside approval, we become disconnected from our true nature.

I had a choice: I could continue to embark on the Anti-Marshmallow Campaign, or I could chart a new course that was aligned with both compassion *and* courage, with outcomes *and* people, with truth *and* heart. I decided to do the latter. I realized that I didn't want to work in a way where I was required to be less compassionate. I wanted to lead with love: to explore what it could look like to be both truthful and kind, fierce and loving, soft and strong. I wanted to live and work in the type of world that allowed for both. I wanted to do my tiny part to *create* a world that allowed for both.

This moment was one of my most significant spiritual tornados of leadership. It forced me to consider how I wanted to show up as a leader and what felt true for me. It also forced me to examine the conflict between the external feedback that I was receiving from a leader who I respected, and my own internal truth. It was a conundrum.

Have you found yourself navigating a reckoning of your own, attempting to make sense of external feedback, guidance, or requests that clashed with your own inner truth, knowing, or integrity? Have you ever found yourself standing at a crossroads, asking:

- Who do I want to be?
- What does integrity look like for me?
- What feels true in my core?
- What if these answers aren't aligned with who others are asking me to be?
- What on earth do I do *now*?

If so, you aren't alone. These are the types of quandaries that many of us find ourselves in as leaders. And they are precisely the types of questions that we will continue to explore together in this book.

To this day, I am immensely grateful for this feedback and for the leader who shared it with me, as it helped to propel me toward the path I'm on today. At the time, leading with compassion was still, in many ways, a radical idea. This was before the era of Brené Brown and the widespread conversations about vulnerability and courage at work.

Today, it is refreshing to see many individuals modeling a new way of working and a new way of leading. It is heartening to see *lead with love* hashtags and the rise of the terms *conscious leadership* and *conscious business.* I believe that this is the way of the future—and that we, collectively, are slowly moving from a place of traditional power and force toward a place of compassion and courage.

Most importantly, I'm grateful that this feedback caused me to stop and reflect on the type of leader I wanted to be. Thankfully, I ended my Anti-Marshmallow Campaign and decided, instead, to make s'mores. This book is largely about how we can all make s'mores, in the moments big and small, when we, too, are faced with our own versions of the Anti-Marshmallow Campaign.

We delight in the beauty of the butterfly, but rarely admit the changes it has gone through to achieve that beauty.

—Maya Angelou

THE POWER OF GOOD MORNING

Every moment is enormous and it is all we have.

—Natalie Goldberg, *Long Quiet Highway: Waking Up in America*

Shortly after starting my business, I received a phone call from Bob, the president and CEO of a regional insurance company. He was interested in working together to improve his company's culture.

After digging in to understand Bob's goals for our work together, I started the process of meeting with each member of Bob's executive team. My goal was to get to know the team and to understand each person's perspective.

During my conversations, I heard comments such as:

- "Our industry is very old school; we are trying to become more innovative."
- "We are trying to change, but change is hard."

- "It's hard to motivate and engage our frontline workers, so we're trying to help them feel a greater sense of purpose in their roles."

It was one conversation with an executive named Heidi that stood out most. While Bob and Heidi had been working together closely for decades, their relationship was visibly strained. Anytime Bob spoke, Heidi's frustration was palpable.

Heidi shared, "I have been working with Bob for twenty-three years. For most of these twenty-three years, he has walked past my office every single morning on the way to his desk. Not once has he paused to say good morning. *Not once.* I feel invisible, even though I am a member of this executive team. All I want is one small moment of connection, one tiny glimmer of appreciation or recognition, or some sort of acknowledgment that I even *work here.* I don't get that from Bob. It is as if I don't exist."

At that moment, something clicked. These issues, described as complicated culture problems, were rooted in connection. Specifically, they were rooted in connection during these small but meaningful micromoments, such as the handful of seconds that it took for Bob to walk past Heidi's office each morning.

We have 1,440 minutes in a day. We have 480 minutes in an eight-hour workday. Leadership happens in the micromoments of everyday work and life.

We can get so focused on the *stuff*—the projects, the tasks, the software, the spreadsheets—that we forget about the people who are making the stuff happen.

Leading in the 1,440 moments, or the 480 minutes of our average workday, doesn't mean that we are continually exerting effort for every minute of the day. It does, however, mean that we are paying attention in these moments so that we can show up for ourselves, for others, and for our organization. We can think of these as small but meaningful moments of connection: to smile at our neighbor, to say hello to the cashier at the grocery store, to nod at the stranger in the elevator, and to say good morning to our colleague, even if we haven't yet had our coffee.

Leading in the moments may also mean reclaiming a few minutes for ourselves each day to do something that helps us to show up more effectively for others. It may also mean encouraging these habits within our teams and organizations. For example:

- Starting meetings at five minutes after the hour, to give people time to transition from previous meetings
- Scheduling forty-five-minute meetings rather than sixty-minute meetings, and twenty-minute meetings rather than thirty-minute meetings. *Note: most calendar systems offer an option to change default meeting durations.*
- Taking a quick walk around the block between meetings
- Starting meetings at 9:00 a.m., rather than 8:00 a.m., to give others (and ourselves) a more spacious morning
- Taking five minutes first thing in the morning to plan out the day, before engaging with technology
- Considering team members in multiple time zones when scheduling
- Keeping a paper, rather than electronic, task list, to create a break from screens[1]

The problem with Bob and Heidi was a case of death by a thousand paper cuts—or, in this case, death by a thousand missed *good-mornings*. Heidi desired connection with Bob, but Bob was so focused on getting started with his work in the morning that he didn't recognize it. Because of the level of resentment that had built up over the course of many years, Heidi didn't feel empowered to advocate for what she desired: connection.

Heidi's desire was simple: for Bob to acknowledge her presence, in some way, at the beginning of the day when he walked past her, through a simple "hello," "good morning," or a quick check-in to ask, "How are you doing?"

This small act, or lack thereof, in this case, represents much of what the research points to when we look at thriving cultures and teams. At the end of the day (and clearly, at the beginning of the day!), team members want to feel appreciated and valued. They want to feel *seen*—not just as human resources but as whole human beings who bring themselves to work each day in service of a shared outcome.

In the weeks that followed, we worked on a few simple strategies that would honor Bob's desire to swiftly start his work each morning, while honoring Heidi's desire for connection. This problem was not solved overnight, as Bob and Heidi had decades of patterns to shift. Over time, they did indeed make changes. With effort, awareness, and intention, they have started to see each other as human beings.

This need for connection was not unique to Bob and Heidi's situation. It is much broader in its application, as I was soon to discover.

A few months later at a scrappy Midwest start-up, I was sitting at a white, shiny table in a windowed conference room. This was a company that many people in the area wanted to work for. They frequently had more applications than open positions, and at the time of our meeting, the team was made up of about a dozen people. The team worked together in an open concept space, with the intentions of achieving and maintaining collaborative communication. The space was glossy and modern, with white tables, white walls, and quirky pieces of art scattered throughout. Most of the team members wore colorful T-shirts from local start-up events.

Two of their leaders invited me to do a strategy session with the team, with the goal of improving communication across the group. Their founder, they explained, was creative and innovative, but not always the best with "people stuff." They wanted to improve their culture and work more effectively as a team.

With my oversized wall Post-its and box of markers, I facilitated a conversation about the company's culture and the team members' communication styles.

Megan, who had been with the company since its inception, finally looked up and said, "Well, I think it's crappy that, when some people go to lunch as a group, they don't invite others. And that when people come in first thing in the morning, or leave at the end of the day, they don't say good morning or goodbye." As Megan spoke, several other team members nodded in agreement.

At that moment, the thing I had chalked up to a fluke a few months earlier with Bob and Heidi had resurfaced—this time, in a different environment and with a different type of company. Once again, the thing that was described as communication problems, culture problems, or a founder who wasn't good with "people stuff" was rooted in connection during these small but meaningful micromoments.

In this case, the impact was especially noticeable, because the team worked together all day in a single, shared, open space. One team member's bad mood or failure to acknowledge the other people sitting around the table created ripples that affected others on the team.

This team's founder, Jamie, like Bob in the previous scenario, was so focused on the goals and success of the company that she occasionally forgot about the people around her who were making these goals come to life.

Similarly, across the team, through no ill intent, the team members had become so focused on their goals, their clients, and their growth that they had forgotten about *each other.*

After watching this issue emerge for a second time, I could no longer call it a fluke, but I certainly didn't have enough data to call it a trend.

That is, until I was sitting at the lunch table during an all-company retreat with a credit union. I was seated next to a gentleman named Kevin, who had recently joined the organization after spending years at a large, multinational bank. He had been in his new role with the credit union for a few months and worked in one of the satellite offices. Over turkey wraps, I asked him how he was enjoying the change.

"Sarah," he said, "it's incredible. Whenever I'm at the main office, our CEO, Dave, says, 'Hey, Kevin, how are you doing today?' He checks in. He knows my name. I've only been here a few months, and I don't even work in the home office. I worked at my last company, leading a major division for ten years, and I'm still not even sure if the CEO knew my name. It's so refreshing to be here. I feel valued and appreciated. I'm excited to come to work. I'm so happy that I made the change."

Here we can observe the power of connection and leading in the moments, through a successful example. Leading in the moments is about taking time to pause and connect with those around us in a conscious and intentional way. Overwhelmingly, I have observed that leaders who take time to connect with others in the small, micromoments of everyday life have happier and more engaged team members and better results. Team members want to feel valued and appreciated. Connecting in the moments is a small but powerful way to demonstrate these things.

Over the years, skeptical leaders have remarked, "Needing constant praise and affirmation is a desire of the younger generations. I, as a senior leader, don't have time for that sort of thing."

Here is the good and bad news: this is not only a desire of younger generations. In working with thousands of team members over the course of both my corporate career and my time running my business, my observation is that most team members, ranging in age from sixteen to ninety-two, want to feel a sense of connection and purpose, and that they are appreciated and valued.

While working in human resources, I had the opportunity to conduct exit interviews. Consistently, team members who were happy with their managers shared feedback such as:

- "My manager paid attention to me."
- "My manager listened when I was talking."
- "My manager was present."
- "My manager remembered things."
- "I feel like my manager cared about me as a person."

In contrast, team members who were displeased with their leaders or who were leaving *because* of their leaders, said:

- "I didn't feel like my manager was present."
- "It didn't seem like my manager was paying attention to me."
- "My manager would forget things that I said."

- "During our 1:1 meetings, my manager was looking at emails."
- "It didn't feel like my manager cared about me as a person."

Bain & Company, a management consulting firm, conducted multiyear research, in which they had participants rank the most important qualities of leaders, choosing from a list of thirty-three items. Participants reported that a leader's ability to be mindfully present was the most important quality of all. Additionally, the research found that a leader's ability to be mindfully present led to increased happiness and wellbeing within the team.[2] In short, being present makes us a better leader, and it can create a happier and higher functioning team.

Simple awareness is the seed of responsibility.
—Jenny Odell, *How to Do Nothing*

We can think our own experiences, as well. Have you ever worked with a Tasmanian Devil Leader? A Tasmanian Devil Leader creates a tornado of chaos everywhere they go. A gentleman I worked with named Nate comes immediately to mind. Nate had a habit of not listening to his team members when they spoke and not replying to any of their emails. What Nate would do, however, was send *every single email* to his team with one of those little red high-priority flags.

This meant that every email from Nate felt like a crisis, even though it wasn't, and that nearly every exchange caused feelings of panic. This, coupled with the fact that he didn't respond to incoming emails, created dysfunction and resentment within the team.

As you can probably guess, Nate had a frustrated team of people who cursed under their breath each time they saw that little red priority flag pop up in their inboxes. Nate, as a Tasmanian Devil Leader, was setting the culture on his team—a culture in which every email was an emergency and a culture in which timely, proactive communication was not prioritized. Thankfully, over time, Nate moved to a different role in which he was no longer leading people and instead was focused on individual projects, which was a much better fit.

If we're being honest with ourselves, we may think about times when *we* were the Tasmanian Devil Leader. Several moments come to mind for me, I will readily admit. Years ago, when I was working in the corporate world and visiting a client in the South, I felt suddenly ill. I ended up in bed with what I thought was food poisoning from the salmon I'd eaten for dinner the evening prior. I missed a full day with the client as a result, which was something that I had never done. Looking back, I suspect that it wasn't food poisoning at all, but rather my body's response to the stress of running around at 150 miles per hour and booking multiple client trips to opposing corners of the country within a single week. I was, unintentionally, operating as a Tasmanian Devil Leader. If I would have been calmer, I could have stepped back, paused, and found a different week for the trip. But in my chaotic way of operating, I overbooked myself to the extent that I ended up physically ill. When we push against our inner knowing for long enough, our bodies find a way to nudge us toward the truth.

Being present is an antidote to being a Tasmanian Devil Leader. Pausing to reflect on the moment before us and then considering what is needed is a way to create a different type of leadership—no tornadoes or dust piles required.

When I was working in the corporate world and navigating one of the more challenging periods of my professional career, I turned to my colleague Gina for advice. Gina was continually optimistic, even in the most challenging situations. She was one of the most adored and respected leaders within the organization, and she still is today. Gina is the type of leader that team members love to work with and for.

After a particularly hard day, I asked her, "Gina, how do you do it? How do you remain so positive and optimistic, even in times like these?" She shared her practice of Friday Feedback: making a point to acknowledge someone for excellent work each Friday before heading out for the weekend. This could mean stopping by someone's office, sending a handwritten note, making a phone call, or sending an email reflecting a job well done and copying the person's manager.

Gina's practice was not only an opportunity to make someone else's day, but also an opportunity to connect to her own sense of purpose, feelings of gratitude, and relationships with others before ending her workweek. It was a natural pause and a form of being present in the moment—and then from that place of presence, an opportunity to express appreciation for others. Most of us have heard about the many benefits of a regular gratitude practice.[3] Gina's approach is one example.

Being present allows us to show up effectively as managers, colleagues, partners, parents, and friends. It is an opportunity that is available to all of us, each day, in every moment.

Here it feels important to highlight the concept of being versus doing. As our list of responsibilities increases and as our task list grows, it can be easy to focus on the many things that we need to *do*. But beyond the work that we do, leadership is, ultimately, a practice in *being*. It is a practice in being the most expansive version of who we are—and from this place, showing up in service of the highest impact possible. This requires us to step back, momentarily, from the whirlwind. Leadership is a process of being and doing. We need both.

DISTRACTION: DOING WITHOUT BEING	PRESENCE: BEING AND DOING
Operating as a Tasmanian Devil leader	Connecting to our grounded and steady center
Playing Whac-a-Mole and constantly reacting to the emergency at hand	Consciously responding to, and proactively engaging with, our reality
Being too busy or too lost in our inner world to acknowledge the people around us	Saying good morning; noticing, acknowledging, and appreciating others
Checking boxes and grinding it out	Considering, "Is this the right box to check?" and asking, "What is needed in this moment?"
Continuously running at full speed	
Tying our worth to our output	Remembering that leadership is a marathon, which means that we need breaks for water, food, and to spot the hills ahead
Heads down, focused on the immediate task in front of us without looking up	
	Focusing on impact, beyond output and productivity
Operating in our own little reality— our to-do lists, our worries, our concerns	Taking time to zoom up to look at the big picture and see the forest through the trees
	Being in the moment and in relationship with others, and with our surroundings

REFLECT

1. What could it look like to pause and say good morning to my team members?

2. What could it look like to shift from distraction toward presence?

3. What practices help me to be more present?

4. Do I lean more toward being or doing? What could it look like to practice holding both?

5. How can I take five minutes each day to do one small practice that helps me to be a better leader, colleague, friend, and family member?

CHANNEL COMPASSION
INTO CONSCIOUS ACTION

What will matter is the good we did, not the
good we expected others to do.

—Elizabeth Lesser

Vic hadn't *intended* to continue fudging the numbers. It just happened. And then it happened again. And again for the next three years.

At first he thought he was just rounding up to the nearest decimal, to make the process easier for the accounting team. But then his rounding became more and more generous—to the point of a couple of dollars per expense. He had been reimbursed for $3,698 extra dollars by the time he was caught. He was fired on the spot and was walked to the door.

Because these expenses had been billed back to the client, Vic had a choice. He could walk out the door and pretend that none of this had ever happened, or he could go through the painful exercise of calling his client and apologizing. He had been working on their project for five years in total, and in many ways, he was an extension of their team. As nauseous as it made him, he picked up the phone, called his colleague Layna, and apologized for what he had done and the way in which he had acted out of integrity. While they wouldn't be working together in the future, he shared his gratitude for the time they had spent together.

To Vic's great surprise, Layna said, "Vic, thank you for calling me. While I don't like your actions, and I don't agree with what you did, I am still grateful for the exceptional work we've done together over the past five years. I appreciate you calling me, and I forgive you."

Restorative justice is the process of bringing together victims, offenders, and community members to attempt to collaboratively determine how to repair the harm that was caused by crime. It emphasizes accountability, and if desired, includes facilitated meetings among impacted individuals.[4] The exchange between Layna and Vic was a powerful example of conscious action, rooted in compassion. Because Layna practiced a high level of compassion toward herself, she was able to extend this compassion to Vic. From this place of compassion, she was able to feel acceptance and even understanding toward Vic, while still disagreeing with, and being hurt by, his actions.

Kristin Neff, the author of *Self-Compassion Step by Step*,[5] defines the three key elements of self-compassion as:

- Self-kindness versus self-judgment
- Common humanity versus isolation
- Mindfulness versus overidentification[6]

Kristin recommends that, to practice self-compassion, "We mindfully accept that the moment is painful, and embrace ourselves with kindness and care in response, remembering that imperfection is part of the shared human experience."

Showing up in the fullest expression of ourselves has the power to expose vulnerabilities that we never knew existed. It has the power to crack us open, over and over again. Because of this, it is crucial that we hold ourselves from a place of care, love, and compassion.

As we work to cultivate compassion toward ourselves, we can then begin to lead from this place—to cultivate compassion for others and for the world around us. When we do this, we can face ourselves with honesty, yet also with tenderness and care. We can learn from our mistakes without suffering twice or three times, without beating ourselves up, tearing ourselves down, or overanalyzing the situation at hand. We can look within ourselves, face what we see, get curious and examine our actions and our impact, and apply what we learn to the moments that we face next.

Elizabeth Lesser coined a concept that she calls innervism. She describes innervism as working on our inner peacemaker so that we can be better activists,[7] looking at the parts of ourselves that we desperately want to grow and change, and not becoming the monster that we're trying to fight.[8]

When we start with compassion toward ourselves, we can then practice compassion toward others. From this place, we can take conscious and intentional action. It is through this combination that we create Expansive Impact—in the big moments that test our character and our resilience, as well as in the micromoments of every day.

EXPLORE

ACTION WITHOUT COMPASSION	CONSCIOUS ACTION, ROOTED IN COMPASSION
Othering: placing labels on other people, other groups, and other ways of thinking, in a disparaging way	Curiosity: What might be true for others that isn't true for me? What can I learn through conversation and dialogue?
Looking out the window but not in the mirror	Looking in the mirror and thinking: What can I learn about myself at this moment?
Making sweeping generalizations	Holding space for the gray and the nuance.
Writing off or canceling others	Having a conversation and considering multiple perspectives
Assuming ill intent and acting accordingly	Holding neutral,[9] and remembering that we don't necessarily know someone else's intent
Pouncing: sitting on the sidelines and waiting to pounce when someone makes a mistake or says something we don't like	Pausing: stretching our capacity to sit with things that are uncomfortable or that we don't personally agree with, before we jump to action
Hatred and vitriol	Kindness and compassion
They	We
Scathing feedback in online reviews or feedback forms	Picking up the phone, having a conversation, and engaging in dialogue

1. In what areas of my work, leadership, or life could I practice greater compassion toward myself?

2. In what areas of my work, leadership, or life could I practice greater compassion toward others?

3. What practices or habits help me cultivate compassion toward myself and others?

4. What does it look like for me to practice innervism?

5. Are there any areas of my work or life in which I'm becoming the monster that I'm trying to fight? What could it look like to notice this, get curious, and consider shifting my approach based on what I discover?

SECTION TWO

BE CONSCIOUS:

LEAD FROM WITHIN

LOOK THROUGH
THE MIRROR, NOT
THE WINDOW

---

*There is only one corner of the universe you can be
certain of improving, and that's your own self.*

—Aldous Huxley

D o you have a colleague, loved one, or family member whom
you *really want to change*? Perhaps a person in your life who
you *know* would be better off, if only they would...

- Stop drinking.
- Start exercising.
- Eat healthier foods.
- Start meditating.
- Become more organized.

- Work harder.
- Get a job.
- Move out of their parents' basement.
- Give their dog more exercise.
- Vote differently.
- Do the thing you've been telling them to do.
- Realize that their perspective is wrong, and your perspective is right.
- [Fill in the blank of your request for this person.]

Most of us have at least one relationship where we find ourselves frequently saying, perhaps with a tone of exasperation, "If only they would..." or, "Why don't they just..."

As a thought experiment, consider writing down your version(s) here or in a notebook. As a place to start, you may consider a topic that you feel heated about (personally, professionally, societally)—and then someone in your life who feels differently.

If only   [name of person]   *would*   [change you'd like them to make]   *, they would*   [impact you know would be possible for them]   .

If only _____ would _____ ,
they would _____ .

If only _____ would _____ ,
they would _____ .

If only _____ would _____ ,
they would _____ .

It is satisfying, isn't it?

It certainly can be.

But here's the cold, hard, and loving truth. We can love other people, we can support them, we can encourage them, and we can provide resources and reassurance—but we *cannot create change on someone else's behalf.* This requires us to let go of our attachment to the other person changing and instead consider the following: *If nothing changes with this other person, how can I create peace within myself?*

As leaders, our continuous opportunity is to search within ourselves and to face what we uncover. Venturing inward and acknowledging what we find can be hard, uncomfortable, and even painful. We must have the humility to keep learning, growing, and exploring based on what we discover. We can think of this as an opportunity to change everything, even if nothing around us changes. This change starts from within.

Frequently during leadership experiences, I receive versions of the following questions from participants:

- What if I implement all of these tools, but nobody else on my team does the same?
- What if I increase my self-awareness and do my own inner work, but my team members or leaders don't?
- What if I go through this leadership experience, but my managers never do?

Or in conversations with friends and colleagues, reflections such as:

- What if I continue doing this personal development work, but my partner never does?
- What if I am willing to go to therapy to look at my part of our challenges, but my spouse isn't?

Reba works in the public sector and felt perpetually annoyed by what she experienced as pervasive incompetence within her organization. Reba was continually in knots about this—thinking about it, feeling bothered by it, and even obsessing about it during her free time and late at night. After years of feeling this way, one day, it hit her: this obsessing wasn't doing anything to change the dynamic within her organization. It was only causing *her* massive amounts of stress and unhappiness. With this realization, she gradually was able to release her grip on this topic and focus instead on how *she* could create a positive impact within her own realm—tending to her own team at work and even starting a side business where she could channel her frustrations into a constructive, joyful, and creative outlet. In short, very little changed at work, and yet everything changed for Reba. This was due to her shift in perspective and approach.

Jeff works in the tech industry and has impeccably high standards. On many occasions, Jeff found himself annoyed by other leaders across the company who weren't, from his perspective, effectively doing their jobs. As a result, he would swoop in and help these other leaders deliver on the outcomes that they hadn't been achieving on their own. Rather than helping the other leaders, however, Jeff realized that the main outcome of this approach was that he became exhausted, frustrated, and burned out, while little changed with the other leaders. After this realization, he redirected his efforts into his own area—focusing on his team, his outcomes, and his division's goals. This ultimately led him to become a more effective and more accessible leader within his own team. As a bonus, he had more energy and time to reengage with his favorite hobbies of sailing, running, and ceramics. While little changed with his outside circumstances, it felt as though everything had changed for Jeff, due to the way he shifted his perspective and approach.

It can be tempting to think about leadership as something we do in relation to others. And in many ways, it is. We lead teams, projects, initiatives, departments, divisions, and companies. That said, leading others comes after we do the introspective work of looking within ourselves. There has been much written on how we can get others to do things—how to influence, persuade, and motivate others through our actions and words. While creating positive outcomes with teams and individuals will likely be a natural outgrowth of the reflection you'll do and the tools you'll try throughout this book, it is not the starting point.

We must start with ourselves, and we must start by looking within.

This means looking in the mirror rather than looking out the window. It means first looking inside ourselves, in order to then create conscious and Expansive Impact beyond ourselves. As Aldous Huxley says, the only corner of the universe that we can be certain of improving is our own selves. We are going to start there. We will practice shifting from focusing on what others are doing and how others are acting (looking out the window) to looking at ourselves and getting curious (looking in the mirror). We'll examine how we are consciously or unconsciously contributing to our own reality. In other words, we will look at how we might be responsible, even in some small way, for the things we don't like that are happening "out there."

Taylor is a former colleague who gossips. Taylor can frequently be found huddled with coworkers in an office or a quiet corner of the hallway, talking about team members who aren't currently present. For many years, I thought Taylor liked to stir the pot, and that gossip was her way of attempting to connect with others.

These things may have been true. Also likely true was that Taylor's gossip was a way of looking out there at what other people were doing so that she could avoid looking within, to face an uncomfortable truth: she had a big, bold, inspiring vision for a business that she had wanted to start for many years, but she didn't have the confidence to leave her position, her abundant benefits, and her generous paychecks in order to pursue it. Instead of getting quiet to hear the inner whisper that was calling her toward her new business venture, she expressed her frustrations with herself in a way that was misdirected toward others. Her frustrations were coming out sideways.

We can observe this in society as well, where certain individuals and groups shout loudly—passionately and angrily telling others what they should and should not do about various issues or topics. Others sit in a place of quiet resentment, ready to pounce at others for a perceived mistake or what they deem to be an inaccurate point of view. What if, instead of pouncing and shouting, these individuals paused, got quiet, and looked inward—considering the ways in which *they* can positively shift their own behaviors or actions, exploring the ways in which *their* behaviors might be harming others or our world, or having a heart-to-heart with themselves about how they are becoming the monster that they're trying to fight? This does not mean that we should not speak up against injustices or take a stand for causes that we care about, of course. Rather, it is encouragement to do our own inner work *first,* so that we can show up and speak up in the most conscious, intentional, and impactful way.

Have you ever experienced moments where you've focused your attention on people or circumstances outside yourself, rather than doing the uncomfortable work of pausing and looking inward? I have.

A few years after starting my business, I looked around the coaching industry, feeling frustrated by what was happening. The industry had ballooned seemingly overnight, with thousands of people suddenly declaring that they were life coaches, leadership coaches, mindset coaches, and health coaches—just to name a few. They hadn't completed any training or certification to do so, and many were in the earliest stages of their professional careers. This trend didn't feel right to me, and it also felt risky for the industry—an industry that has guidelines and standards and accreditation and a code of ethics. I was bothered by what I perceived as a lack of integrity in the space.

But here's the thing. At the end of the day, what those other coaches did or didn't do had nothing to do with me. I could spend my energy and time looking around, getting frustrated, and feeling concerned about the future of the profession, or I could redirect this energy and time toward looking inward to consider how I wanted to run my business, and how I can clean up my own metaphorical house. This redirection of time and energy allowed me to focus on the things that were within my own sphere of influence and impact: running my business in a way that was aligned; expanding my knowledge and skills through ongoing learning, reading, and training; aiming to act with integrity in all types of situations; and serving my clients to the best of my ability, with joy. Ultimately, this shift allowed me to feel free.

When we spend our time focusing on what others are or are not doing, we trap ourselves in a set of circumstances over which we have no control. When we redirect our focus toward ourselves and our own actions, we are setting ourselves free. From here, we can create the type of impact we desire.

If most of us remain ignorant of ourselves, it is because self-knowledge is painful and we prefer the pleasure of illusion.

—Aldous Huxley

It is much easier to talk about the annoying actions of our neighbors, the frustrating behaviors of our family members, or the confounding decisions of our friends than it is to turn inward and consider: How might I be causing frustration for others? What decisions am I making from a place of external validation rather than internal values alignment? Where am I acting with less than 100 percent integrity?

If only doing our own internal work was as easy as giving advice to others!

Author Byron Katie likens this to having a piece of lint on a camera lens, while thinking there's a flaw on the screen.[1] As leaders, our opportunity is to continually remove the lint from the lens.

In her book *Freedom Is an Inside Job*, Zainab Salbi writes, "If we have the courage to look inward and embrace truth in our lives—the entire truth—then we may gain the courage and the credibility to look outward and become a force of great change in this world. We will see our own role in the world we have created. Then we will charge forward for something, not simply against something."

Expansive Impact is about having the courage to look inward and embrace our own truths, in service of creating the type of positive impact we desire. It's about holding what we see from a place of curiosity and compassion, as well as exploring how we can create the changes we desire through our words, our thoughts, and our actions.

EXPLORE

LOOKING OUT THE WINDOW	LOOKING IN THE MIRROR
We first look *out there* for the answers to our problems—at other people, at policies, at rules, at things that others are or aren't doing.	We first look *within* for the answers to our problems—at ourselves, our thoughts, our intentions, our mindset, our behaviors.
We are at the mercy of whatever is happening around us.	We know that we can take positive action, in some small way, no matter what is happening around us.
We use phrases such as "People who do ___ are ___." We say "Those types of people are ___."	We ask "What can I learn from those who hold different views than I do?" and "How can I attempt to understand someone else's perspective?"
We react to what's happening around us.	We consciously respond based on what's needed in the moment.
We are tossed around by waves.	We learn to surf.
We judge others.	We consider how our judgments about others present an opportunity to become more curious about ourselves.
Blame	Ownership

REFLECT

1. Where in my life am I spending time or energy looking out the window? What could it look like, in these areas, to practice looking in the mirror?

2. Where do I have feedback or frustrations that are coming out sideways—criticisms about others, which may be related to feedback, frustrations, or judgments that I have about myself?

3. Where am I using sweeping generalizations about people "out there?" What could it look like to get curious?

4. In what dimensions of work or life am I avoiding going inward? What feels scary about doing so?

5. What is one dimension of myself that I'd like to explore further, by looking in the mirror?

VALUES ARE CHOICES
AND ACTIONS

How we spend our days is, of course, how we spend our lives.
What we do with this hour, and that one, is what we are doing.

—Annie Dillard

T rey saw the writing on the wall. One by one, each of the more outspoken division leads was being replaced. The replacement, in each case, was someone who would implement the vision of the CEO, without asking questions, even if it meant a subpar outcome for customers. Trey knew that he had a choice: he could either attempt to become someone who would agree without speaking up about possible considerations to stay in his role, or he could stay true to his value of honesty by voicing potential considerations and alternative points of view, even if doing so was unpopular.

First, Trey tried the former. He kept his head down, refrained from asking questions and raising concerns, and focused quietly on the tasks in front of him. Eventually, however, he started to experience a fracture within himself; he was betraying his own set of values to fit into his external circumstances. While Trey tried to push forward, he realized that he was starting to abandon his true nature, and in doing so, he wasn't having the type of positive impact he desired. After a few months, Trey found a role within a new organization where the executive team not only accepted but invited and prioritized a healthy level of respectful discourse and debate, in service of moving toward the best possible outcomes for all.

A misalignment of values is an experience that many of us will face at some point. This could be a misalignment of values within ourselves, where we recognize a discrepancy between what we value and what we do—the actions we take, the way we speak, or how we spend our time, energy, or money. This could also be a misalignment between our internal values and our external context—for example, when our individual values clash with the values of our team, division, organization, industry, community, political party, or geographic area.

We will likely find ourselves faced with hard choices about how to live our values through our actions—even when it is hard, even when it isn't popular, even when it means going against the crowd, and even when it means risking everything. We will have countless opportunities to consider: What do I value, and as a result, what should I do in this moment?

The first step is to clarify what our values *are*. Values are reflections of the type of person we want to be, expressed by the choices we make and the actions we take.

In other words, values are choices and actions, in service of what matters most.

Everyday choices and actions are microlevel votes for either the type of person we want to be or the type of person we don't. Honoring our values through our actions is casting a vote for our highest self. Within our organizations, we cast votes for the type of culture we want to create, through values-based actions. Company culture is the collective expression of how employees act, speak, and behave. A company culture will likely form whether it was planned or not. Identifying, and then acting in alignment with, our organizational values is a first step toward intentional company culture.

As leaders, each choice we make, each action we take, and each dollar we spend is an opportunity to act in alignment with our values.

If our highest self is vibrant and values well-being, each time we go for a walk, we are voting for the healthy and vibrant version of ourselves by honoring our value of health. If our highest self is someone who is kind and compassionate, each time we pause to listen to one of our team members, we cast a vote for the compassionate version of ourselves, honoring our value of empathy.

On the flip side, if we have a value of health but continually cancel and reschedule our daily walk to answer one more email, as you saw Cecilia do earlier in the book, we are casting a vote *against* our highest self.

If we have a value of empathy but stretch ourselves so thin that we find ourselves burned out and snapping at our team members or our partner, we are casting a vote against our highest self each time we get to the point of burnout and end up abandoning our value of empathy.

What can you do when you're already doing everything? The problem with "everything" is that it ends up looking an awful lot like nothing: just one long haze of frantic activity, with all the meaning sheared away.

—Katherine May

By getting crystal clear on what matters to us, we can choose wisely in the moments that follow. Over time, it becomes easier to continually cast votes for our highest self, even when faced with difficult choices or a set of less-than-ideal options.

WE CAN DETERMINE WHAT WE VALUE
BY LOOKING AT WHAT WE DO.

We have an opportunity to align our actions with our values. In these micromoments of choice, we can ask ourselves:

- How am I spending my time?
- What types of events and commitments are on my calendar? Do these events and commitments reflect my values?
- What am I currently prioritizing?
- How do I show up even when—and especially when—things are hard?
- How do I want to be remembered?

Each moment, decision, and challenging situation provides an opportunity for us to live our values.

Aadya is an incredible leader who builds committed, passionate teams. She had been working for a high-growth company for nearly a decade when she began to realize that the company was no longer what it had been when she had first started in her role; the company values of today were very different from the company values of prior years.

Aadya was faced with a difficult decision: stick with the company that she had once loved or make a change in service of her values. She values relationships and loved the tight-knit culture of the company when it was smaller. Everyone knew each other's names, and people helped each other out. There was a comfortable camaraderie.

As the company grew larger, this culture began to change. Gradually, then suddenly, the company didn't have the same feelings of closeness and camaraderie that Aadya cherished.

Through our work together, we were able to contrast Aadya's values with the realities of her current context by considering:

- Which areas of values misalignment were *within* Aadya's sphere of influence? What were the things that she could change—even if in some small way?
- What were the things that weren't aligned with her values, but that she could accept?
- And what were the areas of misalignment that Aadya couldn't change, and also couldn't accept?

We can use the above reflection questions for situations in which we are noticing a discrepancy between our own values and sense of integrity and the values or expectations of others. We can, as my friend Devin used to suggest, consider the following guideline for these types of situations:

If you don't like it, change it. If you can't change it, you need to either accept it or move on.[2]

After several months of thoughtful self-inquiry, Aadya decided to make a change. Her clarity came largely due to the amount of work she did to get clear on her values. Aadya decided that there was too much that she couldn't change *and* that she couldn't accept, and ultimately that a greater shift was needed.

In another example, Sofia is a high-performing, experienced leader. She doesn't believe in playing the game of politicking, schmoozing, or cozying up with senior leaders within the organization to advance her career. She believes in doing high-quality work.

After several structural changes within the company, she found herself reporting to a new boss. Two of the early pieces of feedback that her new boss gave her were "You need to work to be more visible," and "You need to make yourself more known with this new leader." This feedback went against everything that Sofia believed. She believed in doing good work and in that being enough.

Like Aadya, Sofia was forced to sit with a difficult set of factors: her own values, beliefs, and core philosophies, alongside the ever-evolving values, beliefs, and core philosophies of the organization—which were becoming further distanced from her own.

In the end, Sofia also decided to make a change. She decided that it wouldn't feel authentic for her to play the game in the way her leader was encouraging her to and that she would be happiest if she could work in an environment where her work spoke for itself.

As you can imagine, the choices of both Sofia and Aadya were difficult to make. Both women walked away from careers that they had built not only over the course of years, but decades. Both women cared deeply about their work, about their colleagues, and about the success of the company. But at the end of the day, they concluded that the chasm between their own values and the values of their respective companies was too great.

When faced with difficult situations involving a misalignment of values, we might first consider what we *can* do about the situation:

- What are the things that I can positively impact, influence, or change—even if in some small way?
- What are the things that I don't agree with but that I can accept?
- What, if anything, is on the list that I can't change and also that I can't accept?

For some people, the third list leads to a point of agreeing to disagree. In others, it leads to a larger shift—whether that means transitioning roles, leaving the company, or leaving a relationship. These choices, as well as our thresholds in each category, typically look different for each of us. There is seldom one right answer, as we each hold different values and different levels of passion and conviction related to these values.

Getting clear on our values helps us act with greater clarity.

I navigated a challenging misalignment of values when I took on a new role in a new department. It quickly became clear that some individuals within this department held a different set of values than in other areas of the organization. Here, snark was the order of the day, and for some members of this department, kindness indicated weakness, vulnerability, and even a lack of astuteness. While snark wasn't listed anywhere on an official set of values, it was infused into the lifeblood of the team.

Attempting to connect with my new team members as a leader who had only recently moved to this department, I acted in a way that, to this day, makes me cringe. I started incorporating a bit of snark into my own emails. I did this even though I don't believe in this as a leadership strategy or as a communication strategy in general. It isn't aligned with who I am.

In one particularly horrible moment that is forever burned into my memory, one of my attempts to connect with other teammates through snark via email was forwarded around and landed in the inbox of a senior leader within the company. I will never forget how ashamed, embarrassed, and sickened I felt when I saw the distribution list on that forwarded email. I had acted in a way that was misaligned with my values and my own integrity. And in seeing that email, I was forced to reckon with the impact.

In a desperate attempt to connect with these team members through a snarky email, I became disconnected from my true nature and my own authentic leadership.

I was ashamed—of myself, my actions, and the fact that I had drifted away from my own truth, in an attempt to seek approval from others. A colleague recently shared that in trying so hard to be liked by others, she realized she no longer liked herself. The same could be said of my attempts to connect with my teammates through snark. In trying to be liked by my team, I started to dislike myself. Brené Brown, who researches vulnerability and shame, has suggested that shame thrives in secrecy, silence, and judgment. Talking more openly about this incident has allowed me to process it, learn from it, and over time release the shame and self-judgment that I carried from it.

In another example, I was planning to attend a writing retreat with a renowned teacher. I own every book that this teacher has written, several of which I've read multiple times. The books are abundantly dog-eared and highlighted. I had been signed up for the retreat for over two years; it was to be held in a beautiful location near a lake.

A month before the start of the retreat, I was copied on a mass email, unveiling new agreements for the retreat. The agreements were written in red font and underlined; they were repeated twice. Suddenly, anyone who was attending the retreat would be automatically opted into these new agreements. They hadn't been included in any of the registration information, they weren't included in the pre-retreat coursework, and they weren't designed collaboratively. They were added as last-minute additions, and rather than communicating directly to and with the people who had signed up for the retreat, the instructor sent out a mass email to thousands of recipients as part of a generic email blast. One of the new agreements instantly made the retreat inaccessible to a portion of the people who had signed up. This new agreement, and particularly the way it was communicated, clashed with my top value of integrity.

I needed to decide: I could sign on the dotted line and agree to something that didn't feel in integrity, or I could begin the process of unregistering and canceling. After much reflection, I chose the latter. It would have been easier to proceed as initially planned; I had paid in full and completed the required reading. But doing what feels right is not the same as doing what feels easy. For me, the cost of not being in integrity to myself was higher than the cost of losing the opportunity to study with this renowned and respected teacher.

Being clear on our values makes hard decisions easier. Our values provide us with anchors—for decision-making, for scheduling our time and making commitments, for the language we use in conversations, and for our actions and behaviors. In the case of my retreat, I needed to choose between what I *wanted* to do (go to the retreat) and what I felt was *right* (be in integrity to myself and my values). While this choice wasn't easy, connecting to my values helped me to decide.

Having clear values also creates personal agency. When we know what we stand for, it is easier to show up for ourselves and for others and to speak up in service of what matters. When we are connected to the truth of who we are, we can show up more powerfully and effectively as leaders, because we are clear on the things that matter most.

Here, it is important to note that values not only impact our personal and professional decisions, but our wider societal chasms as well. When we look around at the things that frustrate us, infuriate us, or provide us with a sense of relief or joy, we may look to our values for clues about why we feel the way we do. Because we each have different values, what feels true or right for one of us will likely not be what feels true or right for everyone.

It has been said that whether during a pandemic or a tornado or a recession, we all weather the same storm but from within different boats. Within our individual boats, we have unique values, perspectives, and views of the waters ahead. We can start to see the way in which this leads us to feel differently about certain topics as compared to our neighbors or colleagues. For example:

- If we value safety, we may embrace restrictions and mandates because they make us feel safe.
- If we value freedom, we may shudder at restrictions and mandates because they make us feel as though we our freedom is being taken away.
- If we value abundant solo time, we might embrace the quiet rhythms of a period of working from home.
- If we value in-person connection, we may struggle with working from home full-time.
- If we value conservation, we may feel disturbed by the new downtown condominiums that are being built along the shoreline, impacting the wildlife habitat in the area.
- If we value preventing urban sprawl, we may be in favor of the very same condominiums, because they will allow more people to live closer to downtown and not need to commute.

The point is: we each value different things, and because of that, what feels delightful to someone will feel awful to someone else. What feels like a proactive safety measure to one may feel like an infringement of rights to another. What feels like a welcomed chance to connect in person might feel like a social anxiety trigger for someone else. Typically, our values are shaped by our life experiences. We each have different life experiences and different sets of values.

Can you imagine the ways in which our world could be different if we had more conversations about the unique values that we each hold, the individual life experiences that have led us to this place, and how these values and life experiences shape the way we feel about various issues that divide our society? Can you imagine, if in place of lobbing Twitter insults back and forth, more of our leaders and reporters instead paused and asked: "What makes you feel the way you do?" or "What can I learn from you, even though we disagree on many things?"

As leaders, we can work to uncover the unique values, perspectives, and life experiences beneath the positions of our team members. When we are stuck in a place of opposing positions, rather than focusing on A versus B, we can dig in to explore what we agree on, what values may be present, where we are aligned, and what we can learn from each other. Rarely is it as simple as A or B. As leaders, our opportunity is to explore the space in between.

EXPLORE

VALUES IN ACTION

The table on the following page provides an opportunity to reflect further on this concept. What are your values? What do they look like in action? Do your actions and choices reflect these values? Does your calendar reflect these things, as well? Feel free to fill out the table with your own reflections. Once you're finished, you may enjoy taking a moment to note any trends or surprises.[3]

MY VALUES	WHAT DO MY VALUES LOOK LIKE IN ACTION?	DO MY ACTIONS REFLECT MY VALUES?	DOES MY CALENDAR REFLECT MY VALUES?
Example: health	Going outside for at least 30 minutes every day.	Weekend hikes: yes. Not taking breaks during the week: no.	Weekend calendar: yes. Weekday calendar: no.

AREAS OF POSSIBLE VALUES MISALIGNMENT IN MY WORK AND LIFE

This table provides an opportunity to take this reflection one step further by considering any areas of possible misalignment. What areas of work or life are *not* aligned with your values? And what could it look like to take a small step toward reconciling this misalignment?

SITUATION	AREA OF VALUES MIS-ALIGNMENT	WHAT FEELS MISALIGNED? HOW DO I KNOW?	POSSIBLE SOLUTIONS
Example: my calendar during the week.	*I am not scheduling breaks during the week to honor my value of health.*	*Packed calendar from 8–5, with no breaks to pause, eat lunch, or go outside.*	*Schedule a 10-minute walk first thing in the morning.* *Ask my team members about doing walking meetings.*

REFLECT

1. What are my values? What do these values look like in action? Are they currently reflected on my calendar, or as part of my task list?

2. In what ways have I honored my values over the course of the last week or month?

3. In what ways have I drifted away from my values over the course of the last week or month?

4. Where am I making tiny compromises that go against my values? If I continue in this direction, what is the risk?

5. What is one small shift that I could make this week or this month to honor my values more fully?

AIM LOW AND LEFT

Becoming a leader is synonymous with becoming yourself.
It's precisely that simple, and it's also that difficult.

—Warren Bennis

Many of us end up in leadership roles because we are good at our core job or, in the case of entrepreneurs, because we are passionate about the product, company, or mission that we are building. In my work with teams over the last couple of decades, I have found that whether we are working as a manager or as an individual contributor, most of us have a default way of operating, which can be captured by one of these four natural styles.

MANAGE

You are excited to manage the work, the projects, the deadlines, the deliverables, the timeframes. You commonly ask questions such as:

- What is the status?
- When is this due?
- How are we going to make it happen?
- What is the timeline?
- What are the key deliverables?

DO

You are excited to do the work. You enjoy putting your head down and crossing things off the list. You may find yourself saying or thinking:

- It's easier to do it myself.
- Other people take too long.
- I can do it more effectively than other people can.
- I wish people would leave me alone so I could finally get some work done!

COACH

You are excited to support others who are doing the work. You might have an open-door policy and perhaps even a couch in your office. You may wish that more of your job was focused on coaching and development, and you ask your team members questions such as:

- What do you love to work on?
- How do you want to grow?
- What are you most excited about in your work?
- What trainings are you currently most excited to attend?

LEAD

You are excited about the big picture, the vision, and about bringing others along. You likely feel energized when working on setting the vision and direction, and less so when you are working on the small details. You may ask:

- What is the vision?
- What is our North Star?
- What is our core *why*?
- How is everyone on the team helping to make this vision real?

As you read through the four styles, consider which feels most natural for you. This doesn't mean that you only operate in this way. One way to think about this: If nobody is telling you what to do, and you are able to work on what you want, in exactly the way you want, which of these styles do you gravitate toward?

For example, I gravitate toward coaching. Coaching is a large part of what I do with clients, and this tendency comes through with team members as well. The gift of this approach is that I'm excited to honor team members' preferences for what they want to work on, and I love supporting and facilitating their growth as individuals through the work that we're doing together.

The less favorable aspect of this tendency is that in the past, team members have said, "Sarah, just tell me what you need me to do! This is your business, and I'll support you in whatever you need." There have been moments in which team members were craving less coaching and more management, through clearer directives and requests.

As a result, I know that when I am managing team members in my business, I sometimes need to aim low and left, which means to stretch *outside* of my natural way of being (coaching) and into another way of being (managing) based on what is needed in the moment. The idea of aiming low and left is inspired by the visual of a dartboard.[4] Most of us have several areas in which our default is to aim high and to the right.

Perhaps we can be too soft in our communication, overbearing in meetings, or in this example, too coach-like in our approach even when more management is needed. Aiming low and left is an invitation to stretch ourselves outside of what feels comfortable, in service of landing closer to the bull's-eye. To us, this will likely feel somewhat uncomfortable and even risky or extreme; to others, it will feel closer to center. Here, it is important to note that aiming low and left does not mean fundamentally changing who we are or acting in a way that feels inauthentic or out of alignment. Rather, it means stretching into a more expansive way of being.

In my work with teams of leaders across industries, the most common style is *Do*. Being an exceptional heads-down doer offers many gifts—a deep knowledge of the work at hand and the ability to lead by example alongside our team members. However, operating *only* as a doer can keep us trapped with our head down, grinding it out, and working on the most urgent issue, which may not always be the most important. As leaders, we need to see the forest through the trees. We need to zoom up and take the big-picture view. As a result, in this case, we can leverage the natural gifts of being a great doer, while stretching into the other styles as needed, to create the most expansive impact possible.

Alternatively, we may identify more with the *Lead* style, as a visionary leader who is excellent at seeing and communicating the big-picture vision. In this case, we may experience challenges when we can't easily connect with the team members who are turning the vision into a reality. Here, our stretch might be toward *Do*, in order to touch down to the ground every once in a while, and to check in with our team members on the front lines.

Aim Low and Left to Hit the Bull's-Eye

On the following page, you will find some common examples of how this concept arises with clients. Use this opportunity to reflect on your own version of high and right and to consider what it can look like to aim low and left, so that you can ultimately land closer to center. There is space at the bottom for you to add your own examples.

Reflections to Consider:

- What is my own version of high and right or low and left?
- What can it look like to aim for the middle path?
- What additional examples would I add to the list?

← ——————————————————————————— →

Direct: can come across as harsh.	Soft: can come across as indecisive or unclear.
Act: beg for forgiveness later. Can leave people in the dark.	Wait: ask for permission up front. Can lead to slog and slow decision-making.
Hands off: can come across as aloof.	Hands on: can come across as micro-managing.
Task-oriented: can come across as rigid.	Idea-oriented: can come across as out of touch with the reality of making it happen.

The opportunity is to consider our natural way of being—both how it serves us, and how it gets in our way. This allows us to practice agility: noticing what is happening around us, and adjusting our approach based on what is needed in the moment.

EXPLORE

HIGH AND RIGHT	LOW AND LEFT
We stick to our natural way of operating and may step even further into this natural tendency when stressed or under pressure.	We examine our natural way of operating and explore the ways in which it may and may not be serving us.
We use the same strategies regardless of the context or the situation.	We shift our approach based on what is needed in each situation. We practice agility.
We feel that our way is the right way.	We recognize that our way is one way of operating.

REFLECT

1. What is my natural way of operating?
2. How can I leverage the gifts of my natural approach?
3. What are the less favorable aspects of my natural approach? How might these get in the way?
4. What could it look like to aim low and left, to stretch outside of my comfort zone and into a more expansive way of being?
5. What could it look like to practice agility, consider what's needed, and respond accordingly?

DANCE WITH THE FLAMES

Life is not tried, it is merely survived, if you're standing outside the fire.

—Garth Brooks

Christian is a thoughtful, conscious, and intentional CEO. He is active with his own personal and professional development in the forms of reading, learning, studying, and working 1:1 with a coach, a therapist, and a mentor. He works hard to create a culture in which team members can thrive, while also donating significant amounts of money and time to support social justice and environmental causes within the community. Christian sources his supplies from local and diverse vendors, offers two paid community volunteer days to team members each year in addition to four weeks of paid vacation, and he advocates for a flexible work environment, with a focus on results rather than hours worked. Despite doing these things, at any given moment, at least a quarter of the people at his company are unhappy about something he's doing, not doing, not doing enough of, or doing too much of. Additionally, community members have expressed dissatisfaction through online reviews and scathing social media comments that he isn't donating *enough* of his time and energy to these causes—and that by running a business in any form, he is contributing to the demise of society by supporting capitalism.

This is the tricky reality of being a leader: we have many eyes on us at any given time, and it is nearly impossible to please everyone. As one of the women in a recent coaching circle said, "Trying to please everyone is like holding ten thousand Ping-Pong balls in your hands. It is impossible."

She's right. We will never be able to please everyone. Our hands are not large enough to hold ten thousand Ping-Pong balls, nor do they need to be. This is one of the reasons that continuing to show up as leaders is an act of courage. To be in the arena, as Theodore Roosevelt said and as Brené Brown popularized through her work, is much more difficult than standing on the sidelines or booing from the stands. To be in the arena, which we inevitably are if we choose to show up and lead, is an act of bravery and vulnerability.

While leadership is often something that we aim for and work toward, it can at times feel like a solo expedition, where the conditions are less than optimal and we are lacking the appropriate gear. In many cases, the further we advance in our careers, the complexity of our work increases, yet the fewer mentors, coaches, and leaders we have to turn to for support and guidance. Our trusted circles become smaller, as those who were once our peers are now our direct reports. It may feel as though we have the weight of the world on our shoulders—our metaphorical hiking packs feeling heavy, with no trail map or fellow hikers to consult about the best path to follow.

We will likely find ourselves standing in the fire from time to time. We will see things that we don't agree with; we will be tasked with making decisions from a set of unfavorable options; we will have to choose between doing what is right and what is easy or popular. Leadership is seldom glamorous or sexy. When sharing their most impactful leadership moments, many of the leaders I interviewed for this book reflected on those times when they were standing in the fire, dancing with the flames.

Susan, a creative, kind, and thoughtful VP of marketing who works in technology, shared one of those "fire" moments. "Choosing which employee to downsize during a company-wide workforce reduction was the hardest decision I've ever made," she says. "It was an already small team and everyone was at capacity, so any loss was going to be felt immensely. I evaluated responsibilities and did an assessment to see if there was anything we could drop from a work or project perspective, then plotted out the reorganization of the team. If I were to go back, I would push harder to have that money be removed from the operating budget versus the salary budget."

Bob, a VP in the construction industry, also shares his fire moment. "When I had to make the decision to close the doors on our fourth-generation, 110-year-old family construction company and let go of 150 employees. My options were to reopen the company and fight the fight against the lender or just walk away. I owed it to my employees, clients, subcontractors and supplier stakeholders, and my family reputation and business legacy to do the right thing and fight the fight, finish the projects, and minimize the financial impact on all stakeholders."

Jackson, who has worked as an executive, a consultant, and now an entrepreneur and founder, shares, "We had to let go of about forty people at once at my former company. About half of those were on my team. Going through the process of choosing which people and understanding how that could affect their livelihood was brutal. I chose to handle each discussion one on one rather than telling one big room of people like other division leaders. It felt too cold and easy to hide behind a corporate decision. I wouldn't do anything differently except encourage the other leaders to do it one on one as well."

One of my most challenging moments of standing in the fire as a leader also involved difficult choices about the future of team members. I will never forget sitting in a conference room on a wheeled black office chair, staring at a list of names projected onto the wall, and being part of a team of people responsible for making decisions about these team members' futures. I was nauseous, knowing that many of these team members hadn't received effective coaching or mentorship from their leaders. I cried every night after work for two weeks straight.

More recently, as a business owner operating within the volatile and ever-changing climate of our current world, most weeks provide at least one opportunity to stand in the fire and dance with the flames.

To stand in the fire and dance with the flames with courage and compassion, we must connect to our grounded and steady center and proactively replenish our inner reserves. For example:

- Taking five quiet minutes each morning before work
- A daily walk or run, free of technology
- Spending time in the woods over the weekend
- A weekly call with a trusted friend or colleague

Standing in the fire and continuing to show up repeatedly requires us to know ourselves—not only the version of ourselves that we present to our teams and to the world, but our innermost selves—the parts of us that are vulnerable, easily triggered, hurting or unhealed. When we lash out at others, it may be because we are missing or seeking something within ourselves. When we are willing to look within ourselves, we are taking steps toward a more conscious, compassionate, and courageous way of leading and living, while continuing to build our reserves of resilience and strength.

Connect to Our Higher Selves

The whole thing was caught on camera.

The windstorm hit at 3:00 a.m. It tore through downtown, where the main-street store was located. The force of the wind shattered the windows and ripped the door from its steel frame. It tore off the roof, which meant that the rain saturated the floors during the severe thunderstorms that followed.

Jack and Courtney returned to the nearly unrecognizable store the next morning. Garments were strewn throughout, while a handful of socks in tattered packaging floated in the puddles that covered the carpeted floor.

The walls where inventory once hung were now empty, aside from several gaping holes in the drywall. The seventy-five-mile-per-hour sustained winds had ripped off not only the roof, but the hooks on the walls and the clothing that had been hanging on them. A single piece of artwork sat upside down against front counter, which was now tipped sideways as a result of the wind.

Courtney and Jack felt too numb to move, to cry, or to speak. The small business that they had built over the last twenty years, a staple of the community and a gathering place for many, was no longer. They stood in silence, taking in the damage. Courtney thought she might be sick; Jack noticed that his hands were shaking. Jack and Courtney had dealt with recessions, challenging years, and countless headaches as small-business owners. They had navigated a global pandemic, rapidly implementing new ordering systems to better support online shoppers. But *this* was a moment of standing in the fire that they could not have predicted.

When we are tested, when we are challenged, and when we find ourselves facing obstacles that seem too great to bear, we can rely on our higher selves to get us through.

Our higher selves represent the best possible version of who we are: our inner leader, best expressed. Our opportunity is to get clear on our strengths and this best expressed version of who we are so that we can tap into this place throughout our days and our weeks, and during intensely challenging moments, such as the one that Jack and Courtney found themselves in at the store, or the moments that Christian faced with his team and his community. When we find ourselves standing in the fire, we can dance with the flames by connecting to our higher self.

The truest, most beautiful life never promises to be an easy one. We need to let go of the lie that it's supposed to be.
—Glennon Doyle, *Untamed*

Let's start out by thinking about who we are when we're at our best—when we are showing up in the way that we desire, when we are having the type of impact that we intend, and when we feel connected to our purpose.

Together, we will think back to a moment during which this was the case—a peak leadership experience. As you reflect, think about a moment when you were at your best as a leader, when you were firing on all cylinders, and when you felt effective, joyful, and alive. This might bring up memories of a specific project that you were leading, a meeting that you were facilitating, or a conversation that you were having. Perhaps it was a brief interaction—a singular, shining moment with a stranger, acquaintance, or colleague.

As you transport yourself back to this moment, ponder the following questions. Write down a few notes if you'd like, using the available space below.

- What was the situation or circumstance?
- What were you doing *within* this context?
- Who was around you?
- What do you remember most distinctly about the way that you showed up as a leader?
- What kind of impact were you having on others?
- What specific strengths were you using?
- What values were you honoring?
- What parts of your personality were you leaning into?
- How were you stretching or growing as a leader?

Your reflections:

Now, as we sit with these images and memories, let's go a step further by uncovering a title, a label, a tagline, or a few key words that succinctly capture the essence of this memory. The idea is to name this version of yourself so that you can revisit it as frequently as possible.

One of Jack's peak leadership moments was before the store opened. He managed both the design and the build-out of the space. He thought back to when the store was just a shell, without walls, shelves, or flooring. He had installed the carpet with his own hands; he remembered the proud moment after which he fastened the final corner. He recalled his strength of resourcefulness, his construction skills, and his Get 'Er Done approach—which at the time had allowed him to finish the build-out two weeks ahead of schedule. Jack calls his higher self his Inner Foreman.

Courtney recalled one of her peak leadership moments during the first week that the store was open. She remembers the steady stream of neighbors, friends, and colleagues who came in to shop. Some brought flowers, others brought cookies, and many brought their friends. She remembers the feeling of connection and community—and the way in which she used her strengths of relationship building, communication, and remembering small details about other people during that first week. She likes to refer to her higher self as The Hostess, as it represents her love of bringing people together and cultivating relationships.

Perhaps Jack's and Courtney's examples stir up something for you. What are the words, phrases, or titles that come to mind as you think of your higher self? And what would you call this higher version of yourself, if you were to add a name, tagline, metaphor, image, or label?

Here are a few examples from others, to spark your imagination:

- MY CEO SELF—the one who leads through challenging situations
- THE ONE IN THE BLUE SWEATER—the one who is professional, joyful, and authentic
- THE YOGI—the one who is calm and grounded even in stressful situations

- THE GOOD SAMARITAN—the one who does nice gestures for others
- THE CONDUCTOR—the one who leads multiple moving parts at once

Take a moment to capture your version here via a descriptor, tagline, title, or phrase:

_____

_____

_____

Before moving forward, I invite you to linger with this image for just a few moments and connect to this version of yourself. This person—this expansive version of you, who is showing up in service of what matters most—is an inner leader whom we will work to bring forth throughout this book.

After capturing your notes in the space above, you may enjoy writing down your findings on a Post-it or in your favorite notebook, to serve as a daily reminder—an invitation to not only _remember_ this version of yourself but to _be_ this version of who you are each day.

Here are some tips that clients and colleagues have shared about ways in which they stay connected to this idea:

- Write the name of your higher self in a favorite notebook.
- Place a note with the name of this person on your mirror or desk.
- Change your desktop background to an image that represents this more expansive version of who you are.
- Change your phone's background image to a reminder of when you were at your best.

- Share the name of your most expansive self with a friend, a mentor, or coach, so that these trusted people can help you continue to bring this person forth.
- Change your passwords to a word or phrase that your higher self would say.

Don't worry about getting the name or the title perfect. What matters is that the language makes sense to you; it doesn't have to make sense to anyone else. This belongs to you and you alone.

Jack and Courtney looked around the demolished store and then back at each other. They each drifted away for a few moments as they thought about the early days of the business and reflected on their higher leadership selves. Jack connected to his higher self of the Inner Foreman and the foreman's favorite motto of *Get 'Er Done.* Courtney connected to her higher self of The Hostess and her motto of *Community and Connection.* They decided that they should probably get to work. As they waded through the water to attempt to find the shop vac, they looked up to find their neighbor Janae standing in the now-nonexistent doorway—currently a dilapidated frame made of dented steel. Janae held three coffees, three blueberry muffins, a box of rags, a hose for draining out some of the water, and a portable speaker. "I thought you two could use some help," she said.

In that moment, Jack, Courtney, and Janae were overcome with emotion—realizing that even in the mess, they had the resources within to get them through. With Tom Petty's *Greatest Hits* playing in the background and their higher selves in the foreground, they together started picking up the pieces.

Barriers and Obstacles to Our Higher Self

Humans are messy, and life is complicated—which means that showing up at our best 100 percent of the time isn't likely or realistic. So while perfection isn't the goal, we can start to get curious about—and become mindful of—the obstacles that get in the way or pull us off course. Once we become aware of these, we can notice them as they arise and then shift our actions, behaviors, and thoughts accordingly.

Ring the bells that still can ring. Forget your perfect offering. There's a crack, a crack in everything. That's how the light gets in.

—Leonard Cohen, "Anthem"

We can consider questions such as:

- What gets in the way of showing up at my best?
- What are the signs, signals, or symptoms that show me or tell me that I'm not showing up at my best?
- What are the specific contexts in which showing up as my higher, more expansive self is hardest?

Jack's Inner Foreman likes to see visible progress. He is at his best when he is tackling big projects and can see results. When he spends too much time in the back office doing paperwork, his Inner Foreman isn't at his best. As a result, he likes to alternate between office days and hands-on project days so that he can keep his higher self activated during the week. Courtney too finds that she drifts away from her higher self if she spends too much time in the back office, but for different reasons. She is at her best when she is in conversation with others. Too much solo time, without any connection or collaboration, drains her. As a result, Courtney likes to alternate between office time and in-store time. She loves working the register, since it's a way to engage directly with her customers—many of whom have become friends.

Once we start to notice what gets in the way of showing up as our higher selves, we can begin to make conscious, intentional decisions that will get us back on course and bring us back to our center.

Jack and Courtney both know themselves well; too much time in the back office for either of them leads to a feeling of disconnection and ultimately diminished impact. Both Courtney and Jack can notice this in the moments when they're feeling frustrated or disconnected from the greater purpose of the business; they can also use this information to proactively plan out their weeks and trade off on the back-office work.

With clients, common barriers to operating as our higher self include: imposter syndrome,[5] self-judgment, becoming so busy that we become ungrounded and therefore less effective, working harder at the wrong thing, not giving ourselves a break to pause and zoom up to connect to what matters most, or getting caught up in chasing external approval or validation.

Our job in this life is not to shape ourselves into some ideal we imagine we ought to be, but to find out who we already are and become it.

—Steven Pressfield, *The War of Art*

Here, I'll invite you to spend a bit of time doing your own reflection. Take your time, and see what arises.

Barriers and Obstacles to My Higher Self

Name of My Highest Self:

QUALITIES AND ACTIONS OF MY HIGHER SELF	WHAT GETS IN THE WAY OF SHOWING UP IN THIS WAY?	WHAT IS ONE SMALL SHIFT OR ACTION THAT WILL BRING ME BACK TO MY HIGHER SELF?
Example: my higher self is creative and expressive.	*She struggles to be creative and expressive when her calendar is scheduled too tightly, and in situations where honest expression doesn't feel safe.*	*Schedule two hours of deep work and creative thinking each week.* *Be intentional about commitments.*

This work isn't about avoiding the hard situations or the moments that pull us off course—but rather, being aware of them and working *with* them so that we aren't unintentionally working against ourselves in these various circumstances. As Pema Chodron reminds us in her beautiful book *When Things Fall Apart*, it is all part of the path.[6] We can stay on the path and engage with it in a thoughtful, intentional, and constructive way.

EXPLORE

STANDING ON THE SIDELINES	DANCING WITH THE FLAMES
Checking out when things get hard	Leaning forward, even (and especially) when things are hard
Numbing out	Staying awake
Doing what is easy	Doing what is right
Chasing success	Pausing to consider, "What is driving me toward the success that I'm chasing? Is it fulfilling me?"
Avoiding the fire and the flames by busying ourselves with the minutia	Taking care of and nurturing ourselves so that we can face the fire and the flames while staying connected to our grounded and steady center
Judging others from the sidelines	Stepping consciously into the arena
Chasing external markers of success	Connecting to our inner truth and wisdom
Attempting to please everyone	Acting in alignment with our values and inner sense of integrity, and remembering that it is nearly impossible to please everyone

REFLECT

1. What have been the most challenging moments of my leadership journey to date? What have I learned from each of these moments? If I could go back in time, what would I do differently?

2. What personal practices help me stay connected to my grounded and steady center?

3. What proactive practices support me in showing up with compassion and courage?

4. In what areas of my leadership and life am I running on the metaphorical treadmill? What could it look like, and feel like, to step off and pause to check in with myself—and with others?

5. Where am I standing on the sidelines rather than in the arena? What am I avoiding? And what could it look like to step forward, with courage, compassion, and care—even if to put a toe in the arena to start with?

UNIQUE BRILLIANCE: EMBRACE STRENGTHS AND SHADOWS

When you embrace your shadow you will no longer have to live in fear. Find the gifts of your shadow and you will finally revel in all the glory of your true self. Then you will have the freedom to create the life you have always desired.

—Debbie Ford

J ack and Courtney worked through the morning, the afternoon, and into the evening. Jack's Inner Foreman was working in high gear as he tackled the cleanup of the space, corner by corner. By 9:00 p.m., he found the drywall putty in the back and started filling in the holes where the hooks had been ripped from the wall by the wind.

"Don't you think we should take a break?" Courtney asked. They hadn't eaten anything since 8:30 a.m., when they'd each had a blueberry muffin with the coffees that Janae brought over. "I want to finish just one more section," Jack said. One more section turned to two, which turned to seven.

At 11:30 p.m., Jack and Courtney collapsed onto two foldable lawn chairs in the center of the space, satisfied with the amount of progress that they'd made but exhausted to their core. They peeled themselves off the lawn chairs, took out the thirteen garbage bags that they'd filled with rubbish and pieces of drywall, and decided to call it a night.

Jack and Courtney, despite the unfavorable circumstances, were both working in their Unique Brilliance. Jack came to life when he had a chance to spring into action and focus on results. Courtney came to life as she thought about the community and customers that she would be able to connect with once again when the store reopened.

Have you ever experienced a moment in which you felt like you were having a significant impact, doing work that you loved, and even reaching a state of flow? A flow state, a concept popularized by Mihaly Csikszent-mihalyi, is when we are fully immersed in a feeling of energized focus, full involvement, and enjoyment in the process of the activity. It may feel as though we are in the zone, or that we lose track of time.[7]

When we are working in this space, we are expressing our Unique Brilliance. We can think of this as our highest expression of purpose; the work we feel most called to do; the work that gives us energy and fills our tank. It is the combination of what we do (our strengths) and how we show up in the world (our essence). Our essence is our special sauce—the energy, way of being, and unique fingerprint that we put on all we do. Together, these things form our Unique Brilliance.

We can discover our own Unique Brilliance by reflecting on the following questions:

- Look at your calendar and your task list. If you could keep only the things that feel like the best use of your talents and get rid of all the rest, what items would make the cut?
- If you had complete autonomy over your time, what are the things that you would do, that would both create the greatest impact and bring you the most joy?
- If you suddenly found yourself able to work only a couple of hours each week, what are the things that you would do within those hours?
- If you could work only a couple of hours per day, what are the things that you would work on that would bring you the most joy and have the most impact?
- What are the strengths and attributes that your friends and loved ones reflect for you—that sometimes you aren't aware of, because they're so much a part of who you are?
- If you could delegate or eliminate 80 percent of your work and keep only the 20 percent that has the highest impact and that you most enjoy, what would you keep?
- What gives you energy?
- What are you doing when you feel in the zone?
- What do you most love to do?
- What types of requests or questions are you thrilled to receive from others?

You may enjoy recording your answers in the space below.

We can think of our Unique Brilliance as the highest expression of our gifts and talents, combined with our energetic essence, or way of being. It allows us to create impact, lead effectively, and positively influence those around us. And, at times, it can overfunction, which means that we end up with too much of what was previously a good thing. We will explore what that can look like as we reconnect with Jack and Courtney.

If Jack would have had his way, he would have worked through the night and into the next morning. Jack's higher self of the Inner Foreman sometimes takes over to a point of overworking, pushing too hard, not knowing when to stop, and prioritizing productivity at all costs. On more than one occasion, Courtney has found Jack passed out and sound asleep on the office chair in the back after a busy day. Jack regularly pushes himself to a point of exhaustion.

We can see how Jack's Inner Foreman and his strength of *Get 'Er Done* has many gifts. And, in this example, we can see how these strengths sometimes lead Jack to a place of fatigue, exhaustion, and even collapse. This is the idea of overfunctioning: it is when too much of a good thing is no longer a good thing.

Now that we have spent some time reflecting on our own Unique Brilliance, let's take this a step further to think about what it looks like when it is best expressed, what it looks like when it is dimmed, and what it looks like when it starts to overfunction. Many personality and strengths assessments tell us what we do well, but they don't always tell us about the potential downside of these strengths.

Our opportunity is to lead with our strengths, while also being aware of when we swing too far toward a point of overfunctioning. The goal is to find the middle ground. We can think of this as our Unique Brilliance, Best Expressed.

Cori is the CEO for a nonprofit based in the Southwest. She has a Unique Brilliance related to a deep sense of caring. She is a fun, joyful, and engaging leader. She is adored by her team and makes even the most mundane tasks fun. Her team feels like a close-knit family, and she feels a sense of love for each team member within her organization. She brings levity and light to even the most serious topics, while simultaneously creating meaningful impact and coming up with innovative solutions. While her caring approach is a gift in many ways, it can sometimes lean toward caretaking. In these instances, rather than empowering her team members to own tasks or projects, Cori engages just longer than she needs to. In Cori's mind, she's just trying to get projects off to a successful start and be a hands-on leader with her team. However, for her team members, it sometimes feels difficult to form strong relationships with partners, because Cori stays so involved. We can think of this as a tipping point, where Cori moves from being a deeply caring leader, which is a strength, to *taking care of* her team members, which can at times feel like overstepping.

Another colleague, Zuri, has a Unique Brilliance related to planning and execution. She is masterful at getting things done. She can juggle a seemingly infinite number of balls in the air, and her reflexes and follow-up speed are lightning fast. Zuri has astutely observed that sometimes her strengths related to planning and execution overfunction to a point of being controlling toward others in her life, having unrealistically high expectations, and occasionally slipping into unhealthy patterns of behavior that help to create a sense of control. Her Unique Brilliance—which makes her successful in both her work and life—can at times become unproductive and even unhealthy.

Finally, Nic is a detail-oriented project manager who thrives when he is involved in long-term projects with many moving pieces. He gains energy from driving timelines and updating spreadsheets. His ability to manage tiny details and move projects forward is unmatched by others on his team. However, these strengths can sometimes lean toward rigidity and too much emphasis on checking the box, even if the outcome isn't the best it can be. Once again, a growth area for Nic is to have awareness of when he is reaching the tipping point, when his strengths kick into overdrive.

We can notice when we are operating from either side of this continuum: either dimming our Unique Brilliance or swinging too far to the other side by overfunctioning.

DIMMED   BEST EXPRESSED   OVERFUNCTIONING

Our strengths can reveal our shadows. The things that we are excellent at sometimes swing too far. Several colleagues in my coaching circles have observed that nearly *all* of their ongoing challenges within their leadership or life relate to areas of overfunctioning—areas where they have taken their strengths too far over the tipping point, to a point of imbalance.

As you think about your own strengths, consider how these, at times, overfunction. For example:

- If part of your Unique Brilliance is what the Big Five[8] calls Conscientiousness, are there times when this becomes perfectionism?
- If part of your genius is your rational, logical mind, are there times when this leans toward being critical, being less in tune to other people's emotions, or doing what Adam Grant describes as logic bullying?
- If you have a remarkable ability to close deals, are there times when you move toward striving, competing, or continuing to spin deals in your head at inappropriate times—while spending time with family, or on a date with a loved one?
- If you are excellent at identifying potential risks, does this ever show up as catastrophizing or shooting down other people's ideas?

On the flip side, there are times when we dim our Unique Brilliance. For example, colleagues with sharp, fast minds find that their natural strengths can't shine through when they don't have enough challenging things to dig into. Other clients who are masterful at asking the questions that nobody else is willing to ask may find that their gifts are dimmed when they stay silent in a meeting, rather than speaking up to ask the questions that they'd like to voice.

I'll invite you to think about this question for yourself.

BEST EXPRESSED:

- What is your Unique Brilliance?
- What does this look like when it is best expressed?
- How are you showing up as a leader when you're operating from your Unique Brilliance?
- What type of impact is possible from here?

DIMMED:

- What does this look like for you?
- What are the conditions, situations, or circumstances under which your brilliance sometimes becomes dimmed? (*For example, some clients find that their strengths become dimmed or dulled in the presence of certain people—or situations in which they don't feel a high degree of psychological safety.*)
- What clues tell you that your strengths are dimmed?

OVERFUNCTIONING:

- How does your Unique Brilliance overfunction at times? What does it look like, feel like, or morph into? How do you know? What are the signs, signals, and clues?
- What are the conditions, situations, or circumstances under which you rely too much on your Unique Brilliance? (*For example, many clients find that being stressed or too busy can be a trigger.*)

Here is some space to map out your Unique Brilliance on the continuum below, along with what it looks like when it is dimmed or when it overfunctions.⁹ Feel free to record all areas that come to mind.

DIMMED   BEST EXPRESSED   OVERFUNCTIONING

Over years of working one on one with leadership and executive coaching clients, as well as in group settings with teams and organizations, I have found that overwhelmingly, our less favorable qualities can be our Unique Brilliance going into overdrive. The sales leader who steamrolls her entire team during internal meetings is taking her brilliance of being results-oriented to a place of being controlling, dominating, and harsh.

The highly creative founder who is confusing her team with a new idea every ten minutes is experiencing her brilliance of creativity, vision, and enthusiasm expressing in a way that feels unfocused, erratic, and disconnected from her team on the ground. Her strengths have gone into overdrive.

The teacher who cares so much about his students that he organizes food drives, outdoor gardening classes, and talent nights but ends up exhausted and considering a career change has swung too far, to the point of *taking care of* instead of *caring for*, which has led him to a point of fatigue and burnout.

Not only can our strengths sometimes go into overdrive, but occasionally we may rely on our Unique Brilliance as a coping strategy, or as a comfortable place to fall back on, even if it isn't what best serves the situation at hand. A classic example is avoiding frustrations at home by leaning into our ability to get things done at work. Quickly, this can evolve into overworking and late nights. Leaning into our strengths at work provides an escape mechanism for avoiding our challenges at home.

In another example, we settle too far into our strength of kindness to avoid having the difficult conversation that needs to happen with our team member. At times, I have relied too much on my strength of compassion to the point that I failed to set healthy boundaries, and, in a couple of extreme examples, tolerated verbal abuse from colleagues. Rather than putting a stop to the behavior, I skipped straight to compassion, assuming that the individual must be going through something hard and that they were hurting. While this approach can be helpful in many cases, in these extreme examples, this was not actually what the situation needed. I relied too much on my strength because I didn't have the courage to do what was needed, which would have been to speak my truth and walk away. Our opportunity is to aim for a middle path, where our strengths are fully illuminated, but not to the point that they keep other parts of ourselves or our lives in the shadows.

At 11:47 p.m., Jack and Courtney officially turned the lights off. While they couldn't lock the door behind them since there was no longer a door to lock, they pulled a piece of plywood across the gap where the door had once been. As they peered inside, they took in the progress: the floor was now clear of water and free of glass shards, and the salvageable metal hooks had been returned to the wall. They had a long way to go to get back to business as usual, but they knew that they had the resources within them to make it happen. Jack hammered a few quick nails into the plywood so that it could serve as a door for the evening, and in a moment that felt like part impulse and part overwhelming hunger, they decided to grab a late-night slice of pizza from the restaurant next door. Between ravished bites, they knocked their pieces of crust together in a toast of solidarity. "We've got this," they said between bites. And they did.

EXPLORE

As you reflect on these ideas, feel free to highlight any items on this list that ring true for you. There is space to add your own at the bottom. These are commonly identified continuums for clients and colleagues. As with many of the concepts we are exploring together, the invitation is to work toward a balanced approach, which takes the middle path.

←--→

DIMMED	BEST EXPRESSED	OVER-FUNCTIONING
Uninspired, un-enthused, lacking an outlet or channel for the creativity	Creativity	All ideas, no execution
Lack of challenge, not enough interesting things to work on	Execution and getting things done	Taskmaster, grinding, checking the box at all costs, micromanaging, burnout
Silence, disengagement	Willingness to ask the hard questions	Putting others on the defensive, throwing up roadblocks
Isolation, loneliness, lack of connection	A focus on relationships	People pleasing, codependency, taking care of, rescuing, lacking boundaries
Sticking to what is safe or known	Ability to see the future vision and what is possible	We want the vision for others more than they want it for themselves

DIMMED	BEST EXPRESSED	OVER-FUNCTIONING
Settling, defeat, sadness	High standards and an eye for excellence	Critical, ruthless, never satisfied
Apathy	Deep caring and passion	Feeling like others aren't doing enough, spraying the firehose in too many directions, inability to let things go
Not speaking up, staying silent, going along with things even if we don't agree	Ability to spot risks and potential downsides	Critical, catastrophizing, negative, hypervigilant

REFLECT

1. What is my Unique Brilliance?

2. Where are my strengths betraying me, when they move toward overfunctioning?

3. What is one pain point in my work or life that might be a result of overfunctioning?

4. What do I want to shift, change, or explore because of this new insight?

5. Which areas from the table on the previous pages feel true for me? What additional qualities would I add to the list?

IDENTIFY YOUR
NORTH STAR

If you want to build a ship, don't drum up the men to
gather wood, divide the work, and give orders. Instead,
teach them to yearn for the vast and endless sea.

—Antoine de Saint-Exupéry

t was a gray hotel room in a small industrial town in Ohio. Within, I was eating a cardboard-tasting microwaveable meal while glued to my computer. I hadn't worked out all week. At that moment, with my cardboard meal and my laptop in front of me, it hit me: while I'd created a successful business by most external measures, I had somehow lost my way in the process. I had started my business to create a positive impact, to be of service, and to create a certain freedom in my life.

Like many entrepreneurs who have come before and who will certainly come after, I had trapped myself in my own business—creating such a level of busyness and so much travel that I had neglected my healthy routines and allowed my revenue goals and my desire for continuous impact to take priority over all else.

I had become disconnected from my North Star.

Have you ever found yourself a passive observer in your own life, looking in, wondering where you are, and asking, "How did I get here?"

As leaders, we need to know what our North Star is. Not having a North Star—or allowing fear or external perceptions to cloud the compass—is how we end up chasing accolades that don't align with our higher purpose; it is how we end up climbing the ladder only to realize decades later that we never actually wanted to be on the ladder to begin with; it is how we end up doing things just because everyone else is, even if they don't feel true in our core. Becoming disconnected from my North Star is how I ended up eating a cardboard-tasting meal in that hotel room in Ohio.

Here, it feels important to mention that in many ways I was grateful for the opportunity to be in Ohio; I enjoyed and respected the clients I was working with, and I was doing work that I believed in. And, as we talked about in the previous section, this desire for impact and being of service to my clients had swung too far, to the point that I had trapped myself in my calendar and in my own business. This is often how it goes. We start out on a trajectory that in many ways seems appealing, and before we know it, the trajectory is driving *us*, rather than *us* driving it.

Fortunately, there is an opportunity to course correct by reconnecting to our North Star. When we've drifted away, our North Star can lead us back.

A North Star is a vision for the future, a point that we are aiming toward, a guiding light that helps to keep us on track.

Within your own life, you may consider:

- What is my North Star?
- What am I aiming toward?
- What is the future vision that I'm working toward?

Within your team, you may consider:

- What is our shared North Star?
- Where are we going?
- What is the shared destination that we're working toward?
- Do my team members and colleagues know what our shared North Star is?
- When was the last time I paused to communicate the North Star to others?

In our daily lives, we can pause to remember our North Star and ask ourselves if our actions are leading us toward it. With our teams, we can take a step back and include this North Star concept on our next meeting agenda.

When we know our North Star, we can work toward it from wherever we are at this moment.

Have → Do → Be: A Slippery Slope

Human beings are said to be the only species that, once our needs are met, identify *new* needs to be met. Instead of being content and satisfied, we want more. We wait to *have* something (for example, more revenue) before we *do* the thing that we want to do (spend more time with family), in service of *being* the type of person we want to be (a present and engaged partner or parent). This can be a slippery slope. There will nearly always be more revenue to earn, more impact to be had, more clients to sign. Knowing when and where to draw the line—knowing our true North Star—helps to guide the process. Here, we might contemplate the Parable of the Fisherman—a story about pressure to seek more and to chase something that already exists.[10]

To prevent ourselves from becoming an unwitting player in this never-ending and unwinnable game of chasing more or looking over the fence at what's next, we can reverse this process and flip the equation. Instead of waiting to *have* something or get somewhere, we can start showing up in service of our vision, right now and right here, today. We can put ourselves in the shoes of someone who has achieved—or is on the way toward achieving—the vision. We can *be* the person we want to become, starting today. And then, we can make decisions from this place.

Be → Do → Have: An Opportunity to Practice

We can flip this idea around by starting with *being*. Rather than waiting to *have* something or *get* somewhere else, what if we started to create the type of impact we desire—from right now, right here, today? I'll share an example from my first few years in business, after starting Zing Collaborative. Coming from the corporate world, I had an arbitrary revenue goal in mind for my business. The revenue goal wasn't based on anything other than my own ego and wanting to feel like I was doing something legitimate and worthwhile, which, in my head at the time, I determined would be the case once I met a certain revenue target. I worked hard to achieve this revenue target. At one point, on a random Friday morning, I realized that I had hit this revenue target several months back. Do you know what happened once I met that target?

Absolutely nothing, except for the fact that now I had a new revenue target! I didn't stop for one minute to acknowledge and honor the fact that I had reached this goal or to check in with myself about whether it was the right goal. Nope, I kept plugging away because, of course, there is always more revenue that can be earned, and there is always more impact to be had. I had lost sight of my North Star; my desire to create positive impact was overfunctioning. The faulty measurement, via this arbitrary revenue goal, had pulled me slightly off course. This does not have to happen.

At any point in the process, we have an opportunity to get clear on our North Star, then rechart our course accordingly. We can take conscious action from wherever we are at this moment. Wherever we are on our journey is all part of the path, even if at times the path feels winding.

As leaders, first we can define and connect to our own vision and North

Star. Next, if we are working with a team, we can communicate this vision with those around us so that everyone knows where we're going and why it's important. We can continually consider:

- What action can I take from wherever I am today, in service of my North Star?
- What does it look like to be the person I want to be, starting now?

EXPLORE

HAVE → DO → BE	BE → DO → HAVE
Waiting to get somewhere	Creating from wherever we are right now
Using "if, then" statements in a way that doesn't serve us	Setting goals and crafting visions and consciously working toward these goals
Feeling stuck in the current moment	Creating from what's happening
When I have or get ___, I will do ___.	Right now, I can and will do ___, in service of my future vision.

REFLECT

Within your life, consider:

1. What is my North Star?

2. What is my twenty-year vision? My ten-year vision? My five-year vision? And my one-year vision?*

3. What actions can I take today that will move me in the direction of my North Star?

4. What, if any, actions am I taking today that conflict with my North Star? What could it look like to shift these?

5. In what areas of my life am I currently operating from the Have → Do → Be model? What could it look like to flip this to Be → Do → Have?

With your team, consider:

1. What is our North Star as a company? As a division? As a team?

2. How does each individual team member help guide us toward this North Star?

3. What should we be prioritizing as a team, that will lead us toward our North Star?

4. What, if any, tasks or priorities are we focusing on as a team that are in conflict with our North Star? What could it look like to shift these?

5. How can we incorporate our North Star into regular meetings and conversations?

If you aren't sure what your vision is, that is okay. Sometimes, it can be difficult to connect to our vision. And, other times, despite having a vision fully mapped out, life presents unexpected opportunities or surprises. The invitation is to hold these questions loosely.

SECTION THREE

BE CLEAR:

LEAD IN RELATIONSHIP TO REALITY

ASSUMPTIONS VERSUS REALITY

Your assumptions are your windows on the world. Scrub them off every once in a while, or the light won't come in.

—Isaac Asimov[1]

---

feel like not everyone on the team is equally engaged," Kari said, attempting unsuccessfully to soften the sharp tone that accompanied her words and the visible eye roll that came along with them. "*Some people* never contribute in meetings."

John Gottman and the team at the Gottman Institute talk about the four horsemen of relationships,[2] which present in conflict: criticism, defensiveness, contempt, and stonewalling. From the body language in the room as Kari spoke, it was clear that the fourteen members of the team had each of these horsemen covered. There was a combination of crossed arms, furrowed brows, a couple of eye rolls, and one team member who had pushed his chair about five feet away from the table, attempting to physically remove himself from the conversation.

"Okay, let's talk about it," I said. "Presumably the 'some people' you are speaking about are sitting right here since the entire team is present, so let's have a conversation."

The team members looked at me, wide eyed and in partial shock as a result of what I had asked them to do. They weren't accustomed to having conversations with each other. They were used to having conversations *about* each other, either behind their teammates' backs or passive-aggressively like they were doing at that moment.

"Well, okay," Kari proceeded. "We have these collaborative brainstorming sessions, and we're all supposed to be participating and sharing ideas and speaking up, and Kyle never says anything. It seems like he is happy to just let us do all the work. It feels like he doesn't care."

"I agree," said another team member.

Ben chimed in. "Kyle has been here for four years, and I would expect him to be a more vocal contributor by now."

The room fell silent, allowing the weight of both Kari's and Ben's words to settle. The wide eyes continued, as the team members looked from Kyle, to Kari, to Ben, and back to Kyle.

There were a couple of other head nods in the room as Kari and Ben spoke, along with several wide eyes of shock as team members listened to the perspectives of their colleagues and sat with the impact of what had just been said.

"Kyle," I said, "I'd like to check in with you. How do you feel about what Kari and Ben just shared?"

He hesitated for a moment, cleared his throat, and after a brief pause said, "It's not that I'm not participating or that I'm not engaged. I care a lot about this team and about our work." He paused again. "It's that I have severe social anxiety. It's extremely challenging for me to speak up in these group situations."

The group fell silent. The wide eyes further widened. Several team members were holding their breath.

Kyle had worked on the team for four years. For four straight years, his colleagues had assumed that he wasn't engaged or didn't care about the work. They had talked about him behind his back and made snide comments in meetings. Never once had anyone talked to Kyle about why he was quiet in meetings, why he didn't speak up in the same way as his primarily extroverted colleagues in the brainstorming sessions, or how the group could create more space for him to safely and confidently contribute. Instead, they had made assumptions about him, created stories in their heads, and then played out these stories day after day.

My heart broke in that moment—for Kyle, having been misunderstood for four years, and for the team, having never taken the time to have a direct conversation with Kyle to understand what was going on. The team had created a four-year-long narrative about Kyle, based entirely on assumptions. And, in the absence of open dialogue, the team members felt that they had supporting evidence of their assumption each time that Kyle was quiet in meetings. This is a dangerous and damaging cycle.

Another example: During a workshop I was leading on Embracing Conflict, a participant named Amy shared an assumption about a colleague: that her colleague, Meg, who had recently been hired in a similar role to her own, was too young and inexperienced to be effective. The impact of this assumption was that Amy started hovering around Meg, micromanaging her, and in Amy's words, "acting like Meg's mom." This was, of course, not serving anyone. Amy realized the ways in which her assumptions about age were getting in the way of her effectiveness as a leader. While this assumption didn't go away overnight, the awareness gave Amy a new perspective on her relationship with Meg—and something to continue to work on within herself. Rather than looking for evidence that Meg was inexperienced and ineffective as a way to perpetuate Amy's false reality, she started looking for data points to the contrary—moments in which Meg shined. Over time, the assumption began to fade.

When we think back to the story of Bob and Heidi and the lack of connection through a "hello" or "good morning," we can see several assumptions at play as well. Heidi assumed that Bob didn't care about or value her as a person because he didn't say good morning. Bob assumed that others shared his desire to get to work right away, with little or no preamble or morning greeting.

These examples illustrate the myriad problems with assumptions. When we make up assumptions, we create stories about people or situations, and then we engage with the *story* about the person or the situation, instead of engaging with the present reality that is before us. In other words, when we are operating from a place of assumptions, we are living in our own little alternate—and often inaccurate—reality.

As leaders, our opportunity is to notice when we are creating assumptions. If, for example, we are new to an organization and observe that our colleagues take the *professional* part of the business professional dress code seriously, we may assume that we need to step up our wardrobe game. This assumption serves us, at least for a while, until we fully understand how things operate. On the other hand, if we observe that every interaction with a coworker is tainted by a set of unfavorable assumptions we are holding about the other person, we may decide to work through our assumptions so that we can gradually release them.

In the space below or on a separate sheet of paper, I invite you to write down all of the assumptions that you are aware of at this moment. The list may include assumptions that you have about colleagues, clients, neighbors, friends, or a person with whom you are experiencing conflict. Be both brave and honest with yourself. Nobody needs to see this list other than you. I'll share a few that I've heard over the years, to start.

- Margaret is entitled.
- Aaron is self-absorbed and superficial.
- The people who live in the Jefferson neighborhood are materialistic, and all they care about is keeping up with the Joneses.
- The people who live in the Sunrise Heights neighborhood are down to earth and relatable.
- Salespeople are ruthless.
- Our management team is incompetent.
- Cody is a jerk.

- Our executive team is out of touch.
- My boss is clueless.

You get the idea. Now, your turn. What assumptions have you made about others recently?

Next, place a star next to the assumptions that aren't serving you—those that are getting in the way of your relationships, your effectiveness as a leader, or your own inner peace.

We can go a step further by considering the impact of each of our assumptions and what could be different or possible without them. These questions are inspired by The Co-Active Training Institute and by *The Work* by Byron Katie.[3] Let's go ahead and do this with an assumption that has some heat—one that feels most present and potentially most difficult.

- What is the assumption? (Write it out below.)
- How is this assumption getting in the way—of your happiness and peace, of the relationship, of the situation at hand? (Write it out.)
- What would be different, or possible, without this assumption? (Here again, write out whatever comes to mind).[4]

You can use this exercise in a few different ways. First, you can think through your own assumptions as a practice in becoming aware of them and setting them aside if they don't serve you. Second, you can write down your assumptions to clear them prior to a conversation or meeting. You may even incorporate this exercise into a daily or weekly journaling practice. Finally, you may decide to clear your assumptions out loud with another person or in a group setting—so that everyone can operate in reality, rather than a version of reality that is built on assumptions.

Some client teams use these questions to kick off their meetings. Others ask, "These are our assumptions for the project. Are these the same assumptions that you're operating with on your end? If not, what is different between our two sides?" Several construction teams, for example, have used this process to uncover different operating assumptions between the project owner, the project manager, the architect, the designer, and the subcontractors. This simple question at the beginning of a meeting has the power to quickly create clarity and to eliminate potential future conflict that may arise when teams or individuals are unknowingly operating with different sets of assumptions.

In particularly difficult situations, we may need to clear out our assumptions repeatedly. Let's take the example of Garrett. Garrett led a weekly meeting with a team of colleagues. At the end of each meeting, he would ask if anyone had questions or feedback. One of his colleagues, Sue, would stay silent when Garrett asked for input but then would mumble something under her breath along the lines of "This will never work" or "Good luck with that." The pattern repeated for weeks: Garrett asking for input at the end of the meetings and Sue making sarcastic comments under her breath. As a result, Garrett formed assumptions that Sue was trying to derail his project, and that she was impossible to work with.

As we can see from this example, Garrett's assumptions were based in a historical reality. Sue *did* indeed make these comments at the end of each meeting; Sue *was* arguably being difficult to work with. As a result, Garrett showed up on edge, frustrated before the meeting even began.

Because they were based in a historical reality and because the assumptions were so strong, Garrett found that he needed to clear his assumptions every single week, prior to each meeting with Sue. He found that, while Sue's behavior didn't change immediately, *he* felt freer and more effective as a leader. By clearing his assumptions, he was no longer arriving at the meeting feeling frustrated before it started. He was free to lead the meeting and facilitate the conversation to the best of his ability. He also found that this change in attitude and approach allowed him to more effectively engage with Sue and that eventually she stopped making these comments at the end of each meeting. The result was not instant, but it was impactful.

Let's explore one final example, which comes from a group in the manufacturing industry. In this example, Eli, a project lead, shared an assumption that he holds about his client counterpart, Gary. "Gary is an asshole," Eli said confidently. Others in the room chimed in. "He's right," several others said passionately. "Gary really *is* an asshole. This is not just an assumption."

The group continued to nod, in a collective moment of solidarity. For the next thirty minutes, we worked to unpack the assumption about Gary being an asshole. This assumption was deeply ingrained, not only by Eli but by about half the people in the room—essentially, anyone who had ever worked with Gary. As we worked through the assumption, Eli had a realization.

Whenever Eli had a meeting with Gary, he started his day feeling stressed and tense. He found that he was even short with his wife and kids before work on any day that he was scheduled to talk with Gary. As we examined Eli's assumptions, he realized that his assumptions were only making *him* unhappy and that in some ways, they had nothing to do with what Gary did or did not do. In other words, even though the assumptions were *about* Gary, they were making Eli miserable. As was the case with Sue, Gary's behavior didn't change immediately as a result of Eli clearing his assumptions. But what *did* happen was that Eli was able to show up more effectively, feeling more positive, and ultimately feeling more in control—throughout his day and during his interactions with Gary. Over time, slowly, as a result, their dynamic began to shift. These examples bring us back to the idea that we explored earlier: as leaders, we can create significant positive change by changing our thoughts, our actions, and our approach, even if little appears to change with our circumstances or with other people.

Here, it feels important to mention that we don't just bring our assumptions to work. If we look around, we will see many assumptions.

- People who are part of this political party are [fill in the blank].
- People who support these types of policies are [fill in the blank].
- People who choose to do this thing are [fill in the blank].
- People who choose not to do this thing are [fill in the blank].

These societal, collective assumptions have the power to destroy friendships, relationships, and communities. Assumptions take us away from connection, conversation, and understanding. They move us toward division and separation. Here, let us pause to courageously examine the assumptions that we are holding not only about friends, loved ones, or colleagues—but about people "out there" in the world. How might our own assumptions be contributing to division, separation, and polarization in our world?

Clearing our assumptions allows us to open our hearts and our minds to others and to what is possible. Removing our assumptions allows us to be surprised and delighted by the reality that unfolds before us. When we work to rid ourselves of assumptions, we move closer to truth and a feeling of inner peace.

EXPLORE

ASSUMPTIONS	REALITY
Engaging in a past or future version of reality, which may be subject to our creative interpretations	Engaging in the moment that is before us—right here, right now
Engaging with the stories that are in our head	Engaging with the reality that is unfolding before us
Assuming that the present and future will be the same as the past	Allowing ourselves to be surprised and delighted by the current moment

REFLECT

1. What assumptions am I currently holding that aren't serving me?

2. What assumptions am I holding about people who have viewpoints that are different from my own—perhaps people who are associated with a different political party, or people who have an opposing view on a heated societal issue? How are these assumptions be contributing to division and even polarization?

3. How are my assumptions getting in the way of my leadership?

4. How are my assumptions getting in the way of my own feelings of freedom and joy?

5. What assumptions are we unintentionally perpetuating within our team or organization? What potential damage is this causing?

FACT CHECK
YOUR STORIES

A thought is harmless unless we believe it. It's not our thoughts, but our attachment to our thoughts, that causes suffering. Attaching to a thought means believing that it's true, without inquiring. A belief is a thought that we've been attaching to, often for years.

—Byron Katie

P aula is smart, talented, and successful. One afternoon, she dropped me a note to let me know that she'd made a mistake at work, and she was afraid of getting fired. While the mistake she made was tiny, within only twenty minutes, she had convinced herself that she was doomed.

We worked together to distinguish what was *true* and what was a story in her head—the work of an inner saboteur. You can do this, too, by examining and challenging your thoughts. Using Paula's example as a guide, let's explore further.

- What, if anything, was *true*? What was true in Paula's case is that Paula had made a small mistake.
- What is the helpful information from within this truth? It was helpful to have learned what to do differently next time.
- What is *not* true? Paula was not about to be fired. In fact, she was about to get a promotion.
- What can I release or let go of? Paula could release the idea that she was going to get fired and that she was doomed.

We can use this process to move away from inner fiction and storytelling, toward a place of fact-based reality.

When we are feeling stressed out, spiraling, or stuck, it is possible that we are caught in a loop of storytelling. Most of us have a handful of favorite stories that we tell ourselves that aren't true or useful. We can call these *saboteurs, gremlins*, or *thinking traps*. Michael Singer, in his book *The Untethered Soul*, calls this voice "the roommate." Whatever we call them, they are little visitors in our heads that keep us trapped in our thoughts and keep us away from creating the type of impact we desire. Common saboteurs, gremlins, and thinking traps that I observe with clients include:

- My worth as a person is dependent on my [productivity, success, results].
- I'm not _____ enough [smart, experienced, talented, whatever descriptor you choose].
- It's not practical.
- But I *should* do _____ [something that's more practical, something that is more common, something that my colleagues, family, or friends would want me to do].
- What will everyone think?

Reflect on your own saboteurs, gremlins, and thinking traps. Who are your unhelpful roommates? What name would you give them, and what do they say? Examples of saboteurs that others have shared include: Judge

Judy (the one who judges every move we make); The Critical Parent (the one who is never satisfied); The Excuse Maker (the one who is *very* skillful at coming up with excuses against exercising, taking risks, or engaging with our healthy habits); The Perfectionist (the one for whom everything needs to be perfect).

NAME OF YOUR SABOTEUR, GREMLIN, OR THINKING TRAP	STORIES THAT THEY TELL AND MESSAGES THAT THEY SHARE
Example: Judge Judy	*You're not smart enough, good enough, or competent enough.*

The invitation is not to judge these or make them wrong. Instead, we can get curious about them, unpack them, and see what we can learn from them. There may be a grain of truth or a lesson to be learned from somewhere within; our opportunity is to peel back the layers of the onion to find the wisdom underneath.

In addition to the assumption-clearing and truth-seeking frameworks above, we can use two powerful questions to check in with ourselves when we feel that we are operating in some sort of alternate reality.

"Is it true?"

And "Can we be *certain* that it's true?"

These questions are inspired by Byron Katie, who came up with a process called *The Work*. It is a process for interrogating our own thoughts. I personally find that these two questions can be game changing; we can keep them in our back pocket and revisit them throughout our days. Let's consider these examples:

My neighbor keeps blowing his leaves with his leaf blower into my freshly raked yard. He must be doing this on purpose—how can he not see that this is happening?

- Is it true? Yes, he's blowing his leaves into my yard.
- Can I be certain that it's true? No, I suppose that he is wearing headphones; maybe he does not realize it's happening.

My client is on a power trip.

- Is it true? Yes, he's asking for things that are absurd and unreasonable and seems to have a sense of entitlement about getting what he's asked for.
- Can I be certain that it's true? No, maybe he's just trying to get to the best possible outcome by stretching the limits of what's possible.

My colleague is a jerk.

- Is it true? Yes, my colleague frequently makes rude comments.
- Can I be certain that it's true? I suppose not—maybe my colleague is just dealing with a lot of things at home and is feeling stressed out.

EXPLORE

FICTION (STORYTELLING)	TRUTH (FACT CHECKING)
We are listening to the voice of the saboteur, gremlin, or thinking trap.	We are checking in to ask "What, if anything, is true from within these voices and stories?
We find ourselves storytelling.	We practice fact finding and connecting to truth.
We find ourselves operating based on a sense of obligation to some sort of outside party.	We operate in a way that we are connected to our own sense of truth and integrity.
We assume that it is the way it is.	We consider alternate perspectives that are different from our own story or version of reality.

REFLECT

1. What saboteurs, gremlins, or thinking traps am I aware of? What do these saboteurs, gremlins, or thinking traps typically say?

2. How do these saboteurs hold me back from creating the type of impact that I desire?

3. What could it look like to practice asking, "Is it true?"

4. What could it look like to fact check my inner stories and dialogue?

5. What is one small practice or habit that will help me avoid making mistaken assumptions?

CHECK YOUR BAGGAGE

There are two basic motivating forces: fear and love. When we are afraid, we pull back from life. When we are in love, we open to all that life has to offer with passion, excitement, and acceptance. And we need to learn to love ourselves first.

—John Lennon

We had just wrapped up a daylong workshop on Leading in Every Moment. The last few team members were packing up their bags, and I was cleaning up the leftover handouts from the tables. We had concluded the workshop by exploring how the presence of love in the workplace contributes to healthier cultures, more engaged team members, and higher levels of retention.[5] After the workshop, Julie, the VP of marketing, walked up to me with a slightly mischievous smile on her face.

"Sarah," she said. "I have to tell you something." She held her red computer bag and her gray peacoat.

"I've started signing some of my emails with 'XO, Julie.' I know that it's a bit radical. It is blowing some people's minds. But it's my little daily reminder to myself that I want to lead with love and that I want to bring a sense of care and compassion to everything I do, especially during this time when tensions are running high, and people are so divided."

Julie works for an organization that is regularly targeted by politicians and protesters. There are security guards at the entrance, and she arrives at her office via two sets of locked doors. Tensions run high both within and around her organization. Julie's email signature was her small personal act of conscious resistance: an act of compassion and courage in an environment that felt divisive.

What does it mean to lead with love?

Leading with love doesn't mean that we need to sign our emails in the same way that Julie did. It does not mean romantic love. And it does not need to feel squishy or soft.

Leading with love means to lead as our whole and full selves. Within our bodies, leading with love may feel expansive rather than constricting. Our exhales lengthen and our bodies relax.

Clues that we are leading from love include:

- We feel a sense of abundance, and that there is enough for everyone.
- We trust in the highest good for all involved.
- We can disagree with others without getting triggered or angry.
- We respect and honor other people's perspectives and points of view, even when, and especially when, they are different from our own.
- We come from a place of compassion and courage, even in challenging situations.
- We are responsive, rather than reactive.

Clues that we are leading from fear include:

- Feeling as though we are manipulating human or organizational chess pieces to land in our favor

- Back channeling, which involves having conversations behind someone's back rather than directly
- Painting others in an unfavorable light for our own benefit
- Putting an excessive amount of effort into looking good and getting it right
- Making passive-aggressive comments
- Pitting people against each other either directly or subtly
- Becoming triggered or angry by perspectives and points of view that are different from our own
- Getting hooked[6] into drama, anger, or other people's decisions or actions
- Projecting our own insecurities, anxieties, or regrets onto others

Leading with love invites us to trust in what's possible and what can be. It is allowing versus forcing, trusting versus grasping, and working to consciously create a positive impact in each moment that is available to us. It means leading with our higher self—the one who is patient, awake, and aware. This is in contrast to leading with our lower self—the one who may be driven by fear or ego.

Are any of the clues on the *Leading with Fear* list familiar to you? If so, you're not alone.

Leading with love sounds simple on paper and can be challenging in practice. It is simple, but not easy.

My friend Tina, a director of content strategy, shared a powerful example of leading with love rather than fear when she summarized a difficult situation that she navigated as a leader:

> The organization I was working for was poised to launch a multiyear digital roadmap, and I was one of the leaders recommending which team members we should hire to propel the program forward. During the hiring process, a senior candidate emerged who had been leading a digital agency.
>
> Her interest in joining as a consultant for this role surprised me,

and it was clear her expertise would be valuable for the program. I knew there was a risk of my role changing massively if I hired someone with more depth of expertise in this area.

I considered whether to act in my own best interest or to hire the best possible person for the organization. Hiring the optimal person for the role won this internal debate.

She joined the organization and quickly started producing high-quality work. As I had forecasted, she was asked to join full time in a senior leadership role, and a high percentage of the team I had been leading shifted to her leadership. Though not surprised by this, I was frustrated and having a hard time figuring out how I could still contribute substantially to the program and organization.

It took about eighteen months to answer that question and find a niche again where I was making a strong impact. The new leader and I worked closely together (and quite well, in fact!) to make progress on the program until I found a new, exciting opportunity recently.

If Tina would have been leading from a place of fear or ego, she would not have been able to set aside her own personal interests in service of what was best for the company. If you've ever been in a similar situation, you can likely relate to how tricky this can feel.

Another colleague, Abby, who works for a large public institution, recently shared, "We are this massive institution, and yet we are made up of thousands of tiny individuals. Each of these individuals brings their fears, their insecurities, and their baggage with them to work each day. Each of the big and important decisions we make as an organization is influenced by these individual fears, insecurities, and pieces of baggage."

Leading with love invites us to look within ourselves to examine how our own fears, insecurities, and pieces of personal baggage are influencing the decisions we make as leaders. If we grew up with a highly critical parent, are we unintentionally being overly critical of our team members? If we are currently questioning our marriage, are we subconsciously triggered by, and subsequently less patient with, our colleague who recently got engaged? If we grew up with a grandmother who was never satisfied with the cleanliness of our room, are we unintentionally projecting this sense of perpetual dissatisfaction onto our team members and everything that they produce?

There are only two emotions: love and fear. All positive emotions come from love, all negative emotions from fear. From love flows happiness, contentment, peace, and joy. From fear comes anger, hate, anxiety, and guilt.
—Elisabeth Kubler-Ross

A few years into running Zing Collaborative, I had a heart-to-heart with myself. While I was doing work that I loved with people whom I adored, my calendar was filled with appointments and meetings and very little white space in between—a scenario that I refer to as Tiny Boxes on the Calendar.[7] As someone who values freedom as a pathway to creativity, creation, and ultimately impact (a core pillar of my business), this was a problem.

When I got quiet with myself, I was forced to face an uncomfortable truth. I had filled my calendar with appointments and obligations not always from a place of love, but sometimes from a place of fear. I had said yes to too many things because my ego feared not having enough— enough income, enough clients, enough work to justify the idea that I was running a successful business. My ego had a subconscious story about what a successful business was supposed to look like, which was based on a narrative that wasn't accurate. It took several years of unraveling, followed by a global pandemic, to essentially wipe out the hundreds of tiny boxes on my calendar, which gave me an opportunity to start anew. Today, my continuous practice is to say yes to opportunities not from a place of fear, but from a place of love. Despite over a decade of working on this, it continues to be a daily practice for me: a mindful effort, a deliberate exercise in intentionality, a moment-by-moment exploration of the decisions that align with my highest purpose.

We see fear- versus love-based leadership in many aspects of our society. Let's first look at politics. Rather than telling us specifically what they will do or how they will achieve their vision or improve our communities, many political candidates run smear campaigns against their opponents to create a sense of anxiety, doubt, and panic.

Some media outlets and journalists use fear as a strategy to gain more readership and ultimately to drive more revenue. Fear-based headlines and death tickers, updated by the minute, allure readers back, to catch up on the breaking doom of the day.

And of course, emerging from shared experiences such as global pandemics, polarized election cycles, and recurring instances of violence in our schools, our workplaces, and on our sidewalks, we can see the ways in which fear has led us, in some cases, to turn away (both literally and figuratively) rather than turn toward each other. Fear leads us to constrict further into ourselves, while love opens us up to each other and to the world around us with open hearts and open minds.

Creating Expansive Impact invites us to practice humility—to be courageous enough to look within and face what we see, especially if we find that our fears and insecurities may be driving our actions and decisions. Leading with love is an act of courage, an act of compassion, and an act of vulnerability. Leading with love is a radical act.

EXPLORE

LEADING WITH FEAR	LEADING WITH LOVE
Attached to outcomes	Fully committed, but not attached
Grasping tightly	Holding loosely
Our ego is driving us.	Our higher self is driving us.
We search for external validation.	We ground into our deeper truth and sense of knowing.
Scarcity: we are afraid that there isn't enough (time, money, fame, recognition, status)	Abundance: we trust that there is enough
Politicking, back channeling, and attempting to move metaphorical chess pieces around in our own favor	Doing what is right, in service of the greater good
Attempting to prove something— for example, that we're right; that others are wrong; that we've made the right decision; that we are adequate or worthy or unique or successful	Remembering that we don't have anything to prove, and that at the end of the day, we can only do our best in service of the things that matter most
Spreading and participating in gossip	Having compassionate and courageous conversations
Creating subcultures within the organization that pit people or departments against each other	Working toward a cohesive, consistent culture across the organization and upholding this culture through language and behaviors

REFLECT

1. Where in work or life am I leading from a place of fear? What is the impact? What could be possible if I were to release this fear?

2. When I am leading with fear, what do I notice in my body? What are the physical clues?

3. What do I experience in my body when I am leading with *love*? How does this feel different than when I'm leading with *fear*?

4. Where in my work or life are my anger, triggers, judgments, reactivity, or harsh words toward others rooted in fear?

5. What is one specific area in which I'd like to practice leading with love?*

For an extra challenge, select a situation or person that you find particularly difficult.

THE TRUSTED FEW VERSUS
THE AMBIGUOUS MANY

---

*The critics are never going to be happy with you, that's
why they're critics. You might bore them by doing what
they say...but that won't turn them into fans, it will merely
encourage them to go criticize someone else.*

—Seth Godin, *Ignore Your Critics*

"W"hat will everyone think?"

This is a question colleagues and clients frequently pose when they are weighing their options or considering what to do next. Common variations of this question include:

- What will everyone think if I leave this incredible job to start my own business?
- What will everyone think if I turn this opportunity down?

- What will everyone think if I transition away from this job without having something else lined up?
- What will everyone think if I speak up and object to the inequities that are happening within my organization?
- What will everyone think if I come in early but leave the office at 4:00 p.m. to pick up the kids?

The question we need to consider as leaders is: Who is *everyone?*

Rather than trying to please everyone, what if we were to focus on the voices—both internal and external—that matter most? We may find ourselves trying to respond to and satisfy other voices—and there are can be many. We have the voices of our stakeholders, board members, and executives. We have the voices of our team members and colleagues. We have the voices of our mentors, our managers, and our coaches. And we have the voices of our friends, families, and partners. These voices can be loud, and they might all be saying different things.

Our opportunity is to get clear on whose voice we are listening to in any given moment. If it is our own, we need to make sure that it is the voice of our inner wisdom and not our inner critic. In this section, we will explore a few tools and strategies we can use to answer the essential questions: Whose voice am I listening to right now? And is this the voice that is most helpful for addressing the situation at hand?

An important note: It is essential that we are creating systems in which *all* voices are heard and valued, and in which they can be voiced without fear of repercussion, judgment, or retaliation. This is the heart of psychological safety,[8] which we can work to create through our actions and our words.

During a conversation with my friend and colleague Jackson, whom you met earlier, I asked his advice on a tricky situation I was facing. A professional colleague had demonstrated what I viewed as a severe lack of integrity and had revealed a side that I'd never seen before. I was worried about the possibility of this person spreading misinformation about me, about my business, or both.

"I'm concerned about my reputation, and about the possibility of the false information that this person could share," I said to Jackson. "Integrity is so important to me."

"Sarah," he said, "I learned quickly in my professional career that we can't go around chasing approval. People are going to think what they think, and we don't have any control over that. People who know you will know the truth."

I think of his words regularly. We can't waste our time chasing approval. We can control our intentions, our behaviors, our words, and our actions, and we can take ownership of our impact, but we can't control what other people think (nor would we want to).

Every woman in public life needs to develop
skin as tough as rhinoceros hide.[9]
—Eleanor Roosevelt

I've found that with the exception of a select few individuals I've worked with, most of us have at least some desire to be liked. Our desire to be liked is oftentimes rooted in a desire to feel safe. We can look to psychology for further context. The three most common responses to trauma are fight, flight, and freeze. However, there is a fourth, lesser-known trauma response called fawn. Fawning involves immediately trying to please another person to avoid conflict. It has been said that this tendency develops during childhood.[10]

Many years ago, being accepted by our communities was key to our survival. It may feel similar today when we are facing turbulence or conflict within our communities; feeling a lack of acceptance from others can make us feel as though we are in danger. As we sit with this idea, it suddenly makes a lot of sense why, for many of us, it can feel gutting to navigate periods of intense conflict with people whom we care about or even to read scathing reviews from strangers on the internet.

It can be easy to get swept up in seeking approval or wanting to be liked. One client, a VP of a high-growth tech start-up, shared with me a piece of coaching she had received from someone in her firm. The goal, according to this coaching, was to work to be liked and accepted by others on the team. I cringed when she shared this advice with me. While we can choose to act with integrity, to take the path of highest good for all involved, and to make the best possible decisions with the information that we have, we cannot control whether someone likes us or not.

I once worked with a colleague who didn't respect women. It didn't matter what we did or didn't do or how well we performed our jobs; those of us who identify as women would not fully earn the respect of this individual. This lack of respect had nothing to do with our talent or capabilities and everything to do with this particular colleague. It was not ours to own or attempt to influence.

We can control our intentions, own our actions, and take responsibility for our impact, but we cannot control other people's opinions, triggers, or unhealed wounds.

If we look at successful companies and entrepreneurs, we will find many examples of leaders who have resisted the critics to stay true to their mission, vision, and values. Let's take a look at two stated luxury brands, Peloton and Goop, and one professional athlete who happens to be a close friend, Jackie Hering. Peloton's goal is to bring the community and excitement of boutique fitness into the home. Goop is a wellness brand; they consider themselves the "tip of the spear," being willing to try things first so that others don't have to. Jackie is one of the top-rated pro women triathletes in the world. Here, it is important to note that neither Peloton nor Goop is perfect, and they have their areas for improvement, as do most companies.

As Peloton was gaining popularity, a holiday ad took the internet by storm, sparking outrage about the fact that, in the commercial, a husband decided to gift his wife a Peloton exercise bike for Christmas. The criticisms ranged from "The ad depicts an unhealthy marriage dynamic" to

"The ad depicts a woman with an exercise disorder" to "The ad shows a woman who is already skinny being gifted a bike." The ad, and the brand in general, continues to inspire parodies, memes, and general mockery in various forms.

But here's the thing: Peloton has achieved consistent success, with fans of the bike ranging from celebrities to political leaders to legendary musicians. Peloton is leading the way not only with fitness equipment but with creating community; taking a stand for social justice issues such as diversity, equity, and inclusion; and building a movement that, as they say, is "more than just a bike." While they are known for their high-end fitness equipment, they also offer a lower-priced digital experience through their online platform. If Peloton's executive team would have listened to the haters, they would have likely thrown in the towel years ago.

Let's also look at actress Gwyneth Paltrow's company, Goop. "GP," as she's affectionately called by both team members and fans, has made continuous headlines over the years—on everything from the jade egg scandal to accusations of false health claims to her daring choice of attire at awards shows. People on the internet call her aloof and out of touch. But many who know her call her engaging, open, caring, and funny.

Her wellness empire, Goop, has achieved high levels of financial success and established a strong position in the wellness market. She has in-house scientists and a quality-review team. Once again, if GP would have based her decisions on the loudest voices of her outside critics, she would have shut down her business years ago. Instead, she's busy looking at the next way to positively disrupt the wellness industry. She's unapologetic about the fact that her products aren't for everyone, and she's acutely aware of what the haters have to say. She's been insightful in observing a trend in her business: she and her team try something before it's widely adopted, they receive tremendous amounts of criticism, and then a few months or years later, the thing they tried and were criticized for becomes adopted and popular. Rather than fighting against this trend, GP wrote it into her business strategy: "We go first so that you don't have to."

"Being the person that people perceive me to be is inherently traumatic," she shared in an article published in *Harper's Bazaar*.[11] She knows who she is and what her company stands for, and she lets those things—not the voices of the critics—serve as her guideposts.

Finally, my friend Jackie Hering has stayed true to herself and her own values by defying many of the trends of her industry. Where many other professional triathletes have a professional camera crew following them around during their workouts, Jackie focuses her energy on her training and her family—implementing creative strategies such as stroller runs with her kids, biking to meet her family at the park, and alternating between training-focused days and family-focused days. Jackie has chosen to train in a way that works for her and for her family—which has meant setting aside outside definitions and expectations of how things are supposed to be.

Focusing on our own integrity and values and releasing the opinions and judgments of others sounds nice on paper but can be challenging in practice. As a result, it can be helpful to have some concrete practices that we can use to help us reconnect to our own inner compass and release the judgments and opinions that aren't serving us. We will explore three such practices on the pages that follow:

- Writing down the list of people whose opinions you value
- Performing an integrity check
- Identifying your mentors from up close or afar

Prestige is the opinion of the rest of the world. When you can ask the opinions of people whose judgement you respect, what does it add to consider the opinions of people you don't even know?

—Paul Graham

The Trusted Few

Who are the people in your life whose opinions you *actually* care about? Not your competitors or the person who once made a harsh comment that still rings in your years or an anonymous reviewer online, but the opinions that you truly value?

My list includes a select group of loved ones, trusted friends and soul sisters, and professional colleagues whom I respect and admire. The list isn't terribly long, nor does it need to be.

Who are the people on your list? When making a decision, sending out a piece of communication, or considering your next steps, who are the people whom you *would* benefit from consulting or checking in with? This list is very different than the generic everyone that we talked about earlier, and it is also different than the gremlins, saboteurs, or thinking traps that we explored in previous sections. These are our mentors, our respected guides, and our trusted few. These are the people who give us freedom to act from our highest integrity and our wholeness—while also reading through the all-company email before we hit send, to help us spot any important omissions. They're the people who support us in making the leap away from our job of twenty years, while also offering to proofread our resume.

MY TRUSTED FEW

In the space below, consider your own Trusted Few. Write down specific names in the box.

When we find ourselves facing fear, judgment, or perceived criticism, which most of us do, as leaders, we can check in with our Trusted Few, rather than getting swept away by the potential perceptions of the Ambiguous Many.

When people don't want the best for you, they are not the best for you.

—Gayle King

External Image versus Inner Integrity: Perform an Integrity Check

An integrity check is a simple and powerful process that we can perform whenever we are making a decision, taking action, or considering our options. It involves asking these three questions:

- Am I acting in integrity to myself?
- Am I acting in integrity with others?
- Am I acting in integrity to the greater good—my team, my organization, my community, and the planet?

Acting in integrity to ourselves means that we are acting in alignment with our values and our principles.

Acting in integrity with others means that we are acting in alignment through our words and our actions with others in our lives. This list includes family members, friends, colleagues, clients, and partners.

Acting in integrity to the greater good means that we are acting in service of the greatest good for all beings and within the greater context. This list includes our community, the environment, and the world around us.

If we are acting in full integrity to these three things, we can typically feel confident that we are making the best possible decisions with the information that we have. We can think of this as a triple win, working toward a triple bottom line, or a win/win/win solution (me, you, the greater good).

We can use an integrity check to proactively guide our decisions and actions, and to reflect on our days and weeks. We can also use an integrity check to pull ourselves out of spiraling—moments in which we are suffering twice, replaying events in our head, or beating ourselves up about something we did or did not do. An integrity check is a quick gut check to consider: how can I act in the highest good for all involved? As we talked about earlier in the book when we explored the topic of values, an integrity check is a way to make hard decisions easier and complicated situations more straightforward.

In my own business, I try to use this process whenever I'm making a decision about what to say yes to; how to approach sticky situations with friends and clients; and even when making selections on office space or supplies for my coaching circles.

Which areas of your work or life would benefit from an integrity check?

Positive personality traits, while often essential for success, constitute secondary greatness. To focus on personality before character is to try to grow the leaves without the roots.
—Stephen R. Covey, *Principle-Centered Leadership*

Mentors Up Close and From Afar

In his blog post titled "How to Ask Your Mentors for Help,"[12] Derek Sivers shares his process for making hard decisions. In short, he writes a good description, his options, and some thoughts on each. He works to predict what his mentors will say and to address any obvious points in advance. Typically by this point, he finds that he doesn't need to reach out at all, since the answer has become clear. He concludes the post with this quote.

Truth is, I've hardly talked with my mentors in years. None of them know they are my mentors. And one doesn't know I exist.

—Derek Sivers

The idea is to identify a handful of people who inspire us, whose values align with ours. This list may overlap with the list that you created previously of opinions that matter. As Derek highlights, we don't need to know these individuals or have even spoken with them. They can be our mentors from afar.

When we are facing a hard problem or feeling stuck, we can consult our mentors from afar to consider what they would say. It can be helpful to make a list of your mentors from afar and the main philosophies of each and to keep it somewhere that's easy to reference.

The more we grow as leaders, the more eyes we will have on us. We will be judged and sometimes criticized for our actions or lack thereof. Chasing approval is neither sustainable nor effective. Instead, we can get clear on what integrity means to us, whose opinions we value, the members of our internal board of directors and how to leverage them, and our external board of directors—or mentors from afar. From here, we can check in with ourselves, and our list, to help ensure that we're on the right track.

There is an important distinction between chasing approval and honoring the perspectives of all involved. We will talk later in the book about how we can honor different perspectives and points of view through curiosity and deep listening. As we've talked about so far, it's essential that our team members feel valued and heard. Our opportunity as leaders is to make sure we are paying attention and listening deeply to those around us. When we let go of chasing approval, we create more space to do just that. From here, we can focus on the perspectives and points of view from the people who are in the arena alongside us, rather than those who are throwing criticisms and unsolicited opinions from the sidelines.[13]

EXPLORE

THE AMBIGUOUS MANY	THE TRUSTED FEW
What will everyone think?	What perspective might my Trusted Few offer?
Chasing approval	Seeking selective input
Strangers on the internet or out there in the world	Trusted individuals and mentors from afar
External approval	Inner integrity

REFLECT

1. Who are the specific people in my Trusted Few?

2. What could it look like to let go of chasing approval from the Ambiguous Many, and instead to check in with my Trusted Few and my own Inner Integrity?

3. Who are my mentors from up close or afar? And how can I channel their guidance and perspective, even without reaching out?

4. What decisions, projects, or actions could benefit from an integrity check?

5. How can I incorporate these ideas into my weekly rhythms? What about with my team or colleagues?

CREATE CLEAR
CONTAINERS

This is the power of gathering: it inspires us—delightfully—to be more hopeful, more joyful, more thoughtful: in a word, more alive.

—Alice Waters

---

received a request from a colleague in my industry named Lacy. Lacy expressed interest in meeting via phone to connect and to talk about an upcoming conference that she was helping to organize. I sometimes speak at conferences and incorrectly assumed that exploring this possibility was the purpose of her request.

Twenty-three minutes into the thirty-minute conversation, after several pleasantries and much high-level conversation, Lacy mentioned something about conference sponsorships. At that moment, I realized that I was confused. "I'm sorry," I said. "Would you mind clarifying? Are you asking me to speak at the conference, sponsor the conference, or something else? I'm realizing that I am not sure what you're asking."

Lacy clarified that she did, indeed, want me to sponsor the

conference—but had not yet *asked* me to sponsor the conference.

I felt a wave of frustration toward myself. I rarely sponsor conferences. I typically say yes to sponsorship only when the conference is closely aligned with my values, where it is in line with my philosophy of conscious leadership and the triple bottom line,[14] or in cases that involve partnering with or supporting another 1% for the Planet organization.[15] If I would have known that this was the intention of the call up front, I could have politely declined the conversation and, as a result, given us both the gift of thirty extra minutes in our day. Lacy hadn't clearly communicated her intention for the call; I hadn't explicitly asked. In the spirit of looking in the mirror, I had nowhere to look but right back at myself. I had failed to ask the right questions about the intent of this conversation ahead of time.

This conversation was an example of not having a clear container. A clear container is an explicit and expressed purpose for a conversation, meeting, project, or relationship. It is something that we can use to establish expectations up front by taking a couple of steps back before diving in. A clear container allows all parties to be on the same page about what will and what won't be happening. I failed to ask the right questions up front with Lacy; as a result, we were attempting to have a conversation that felt ambiguous and confusing. Our container was not well defined. We can think of this as the difference between a leaky and an airtight container of liquid. The container for this call was most certainly leaky, its contents spilling out in the form of confusion, ambiguity, and a meandering conversation.

Frequently, conflict is not a result of what is or isn't happening or what is or isn't being said, but rather, it is a result of misaligned expectations. Conflict happens when we expect one thing but get something else. To reduce conflict, align expectations, and increase the success of our meetings, conversations, and relationships, it is helpful to create clarity up front. A clear container involves defining an explicit and expressed purpose. It also includes a set of shared agreements about not only *what* we want to cover, but *how* we want to work together.

We can think of this process as follows:

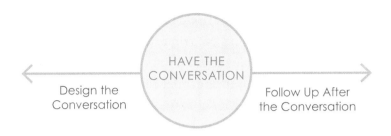

HAVE THE
CONVERSATION

Design the
Conversation

Follow Up After
the Conversation

In short, when we create a clear container, we are defining how we intend for things to go, before we jump in. This includes identifying shared goals, defining desired outcomes, and clarifying the specific purpose of an upcoming conversation or meeting. It also includes talking about *how* we want to work together and be in relationship together, and exploring our shared desires, hopes, and aspirations. Creating a clear container involves taking a step back before we leap forward.

When I was working in the corporate world, there was a particularly contentious relationship between a mentor and mentee, Kai and David. For the entirety of the multiyear project, their relationship was troubled. David resented Kai, and Kai was frustrated with David. After months of tension and complaining, I sat down with Kai and David to try to figure out what was going on. After peeling back some layers of the metaphorical onion, the source of the conflict was revealed.

At the end of each day, after being on site with the client, Kai and David would drive back to the hotel together in their shared rental car. Kai liked to spend that time in the car debriefing, reviewing what went well, what could have been improved, and talking about how David could learn, grow, or prepare for tomorrow. David, an introvert, preferred to have a few minutes to decompress. He liked to end the day with silence, and with space to recharge his battery on the way home before team dinner, which, as an introvert, was also draining for him. His preference would have been to debrief in the morning, or when the two were back in the office at the end of the week.

Kai and David had never talked about these preferences. As a result, Kai would try to connect with David on the way home and found David to be disengaged and slightly difficult. David found Kai to be overbearing and irritating, with his blood boiling each time Kai launched into his debrief.

This problem had a simple solution. Kai and David could talk about their varying preferences for their debrief conversations and then redesign their structure accordingly. But for months, this didn't happen, and the tension continued to rise. It wasn't until the three of us met, after months of tension, that we uncovered the source of the issue and were able to talk through a new way forward.

You can see in this example, as well as in the example of Heidi and Bob from earlier in the book, that the lack of creating a clear container up front can have results that range from mild frustration to catastrophic damage. The process of designing a clear container does not have to be long, complicated, or arduous; sometimes it is as simple as a five- or two-minute conversation to talk through preferences and working style. Taking these few minutes up front has the power to improve everything that follows. Communication is key.

A clear container creates the conditions in which collaboration, conversations, and connection can flourish. In my time working with teams across industries and geographies, with significant correlation, conflict within the group ties back to the lack of a clearly defined container—whether for meetings, projects, conversations, or relationships.

Here, we will establish a concrete structure that we can use to create clarity in our relationships, conversations, work, and lives.

DESIGN THE RELATIONSHIP	DESIGN THE CONVERSATION
How do we want to be in relationship together?	Why are we here?
How do we want to work together?	What do we hope to accomplish?
What are our expectations for each other?	What's our specific purpose?
	What are our desired outcomes?

Create a Clear Container for Relationships

Creating a clear container for relationships allows us to step back to consider the questions of "How do we want to work together?" and "How do we want to be in relationship together?" This can be particularly useful any time that we are beginning a new relationship or when an existing relationship is changing in structure or form—for example, when a new team member joins our organization; when we move from peer to manager; or when we join a new project.

It builds a foundation for all that follows—specific meetings, conversations, and even conflicts that may arise. It allows us to define what we desire, and what we expect, from each other.

Have you ever found yourself four months into a relationship with a new manager, only to realize that you have no idea how this manager likes to work, communicate, or share feedback?

Or perhaps six months into a dating relationship, only to realize you have no idea if this is serious and monogamous or casual and open?

If so, you may have skipped over the important step of designing your relationship—creating a clear container to exist within, together.

Consider these questions to create clarity within your relationships. You might use these when a new team member joins your team, when kicking off a new committee or workgroup, or yes—even when dating someone new.

PREFERENCES, APPROACH, AND STYLE

- Tell me a bit about you.
- How do you like to work?
- What's your working style?
- What's my working style?
- What will success look like for you within this relationship?
- How can I best support you?
- How can you best support me?
- How can we best support each other?

- What do you need from me?
- What do I need from you?
- What do we need from each other?
- What are the things that I should know about you?
- What are the things that you should know about me?
- What motivates you?
- What motivates me?
- What demotivates you?
- What demotivates me?
- What bugs you?
- What bugs me?
- What are my unhealthy habits when I'm stressed or overwhelmed?
- What are yours?

COMMUNICATION AND FEEDBACK

- How do you like to communicate?
- How do I like to communicate?
- How would you describe your communication style?
- How would I describe my communication style?
- What differences are we uncovering related to communication—and how can we honor these throughout our work together?
- How do you like to receive feedback?
- How do I like to receive feedback?
- How do we want to share feedback along the way?
- What is your preferred rhythm for communication and meetings?
- What is mine?

HIGH DREAM AND ASPIRATIONAL VISION

- What do you hope for in this relationship?
- What do I hope for in this relationship?
- How can we work together to move toward this vision?

We can use these questions in two ways: to design a relationship upfront and to redesign a relationship as it grows and progresses. Ideally, we will create a clear container *before* we engage in a relationship. That said, these tools are available to us anytime. Whenever a relationship gets knocked off course, it can be helpful to check in, redesign, and rebuild.

Create a Clear Container for Projects, Conversations, and Meetings

In addition to creating a clear container for our relationships, we can do the same for projects, conversations, and meetings. This involves getting clear on our shared purpose, talking through our desired outcomes, exploring our high dream and aspirational vision, and thinking about how we want things to *feel* by naming the desired energy.[16]

STAKE AND CORE PURPOSE

Naming our stake involves identifying and clarifying our overarching *why*. It's about getting clear on what matters and what is important. If we can't figure out what our stake is, it is important to pause and reflect. If we don't know *why* we're doing something, we can ask ourselves whether we should be doing it at all.

QUESTIONS TO UNCOVER AND CLARIFY OUR STAKE

- Why are we here?
- What matters?
- What's important?
- What is this all about?
- At the end of the day, what is this all about?
- What is our core purpose?

DESIRED OUTCOMES

This involves reflecting on what we want to walk away with. If naming our stake helps us to clarify the *why*, naming our desired outcomes helps us to clarify the *what*. If you are responsible for creating meeting agendas, for example, you may modify your agenda topic from an item such as "updates" to something more specific such as "understand key barriers from each project lead; determine a plan to resolve them."

QUESTIONS TO IDENTIFY DESIRED OUTCOMES

- What do we want to gain from this conversation, meeting, project, or gathering?
- What specific outcome(s) are we trying to achieve?
- What does success look like?
- What is our desired end state?
- What is our definition of done?
- What will be different as a result?
- How will we know when we've achieved it?
- What is the desired purpose of this conversation? (For example, is this to solve a problem? Vent[17]? Air a grievance? Create a solution?)

HIGH DREAM AND ASPIRATIONAL VISION

Our high dream is our bold vision for what is possible. This step invites us to look at the big-picture vision of what could be. We can explore the high dream and aspirational vision by asking questions such as:

- What is the best-case scenario?
- What is the big, bold vision?
- What would exceed our expectations?
- If anything is possible, what will be happening as a result?

ENERGY

Our final step is to think about how we want our conversations, meetings, and relationships to *feel*. In addition to what we are talking about, how do we want others to feel while we're having the conversation? How do we want the meeting to feel for those who attend? How do we want our working relationship to feel throughout?

QUESTIONS TO CONSIDER

- How do we want the conversation to *feel*?
- How do we want the other person to feel during this exchange?
- How do we want the meeting or gathering to feel?
- How can I help to cultivate these feelings?
- How can I mindfully *create* this desired energy?
- What do I need to let go of or release in order to do so?

EXPLORE

AN UNCLEAR, ILL-DEFINED, OR LEAKY CONTAINER	A CLEAR, WELL-DEFINED, AND AIRTIGHT CONTAINER
We are unsure what to expect from each other.	We know what to expect from each other.
We aren't sure why we're here.	We know why we are here.
There are bullet points on an agenda but not a clear purpose or set of objectives.	There is a clear, shared purpose as well as a set of desired outcomes.
We are walking on eggshells.	We are making cheesecake.[18]

REFLECT

1. What relationships in my work or life could benefit from designing or redesigning a clear container?

2. What gatherings, meetings, or conversations could benefit from designing or redesigning a clear container?

3. Where am I experiencing conflict or frustration in my work or life as a result of a leaky or ill-defined container?

4. How can I use the tools in this chapter to improve my relationships, meetings, or conversations?

5. What is one small step that I can take toward creating this clear container in at least one dimension of work or life?

EXPLICIT VERSUS IMPLIED: CLARIFY EXPECTATIONS

We all want different somethings. Some slightly different, some substantially. Companies, however, must settle the collective difference, pick a point, and navigate towards somewhere, lest they get stuck circling nowhere.

—Jason Fried

C larifying expectations can reduce decision fatigue, swirl, and disappointment from all parties. If we define expectations up front, it empowers subsequent conversations, meetings, and projects to go more smoothly. It allows people to opt in or out accordingly. It is easier to be curious and present with others when we know why we're here and what we can expect from each other.

Let's take two examples from two different companies to explore what this looks like when it's done well and when it is not. A colleague Steve recently started a job with a new company. During the interview process, the hiring manager shared, "We are not a fully remote company, but we do offer flexibility for our employees to work from home one day per week." Steve was excited about this option, as the office is located fifty minutes from his home. A few months into his new job, Steve mentioned that he'd be working from home one morning with a sick kiddo. Shortly after sending this note to his manager, he received the following reply: "I just don't want to see tension build between you and the team." The expectations at this company were unclear; while the managers within the company said that they were open to employees working from home one day per week, they did not uphold this notion through words or behaviors. This created both confusion and frustration for Steve, as his lived experience was much different than the words that were communicated during the hiring process. Put another way, to go back to our earlier exploration of values, there was a conflict between what the company said they valued and believed and what they did in practice. Their expressed values and their behaviors were misaligned.

On the flip side, let's look at the example of another company—a high-growth tech start-up with a remote-first work environment. This company is clear with its expectations: *We are a remote-first company, which means you can live and work from anywhere you want. What matters is not where you work from, but the quality of the work that you do. We evaluate performance based on results, not based on "butts in seats." Work from wherever makes you feel most productive. Wear whatever you want. We trust you.*

The expectations here are clear: we are not going to micromanage when you work, where you work from, or what you wear, but we do expect you to accomplish great work. This allows employees to take a collective exhale. They know what is expected and how to be successful. The expectations are explicit, expressed, and regularly talked about during team meetings.

We can work to create clarity within the everyday rhythms of our life as well. For example, if we are planning a family trip, is this a trip, or a vacation?[19] Is this meant to be an adventure-packed set of days where we are hiking in the mountains and taking in the sights, or is this meant to be a complete recharge during which we are lounging on the beach? Similarly, when balancing the schedules of two working parents and kids' daycare schedules, who is on daycare pickup, and when? And rather than waiting until we are in a bind, we can talk through, in a partnership, potentially challenging situations such as what we will do when both parents need to work late, but daycare closes early.

It has been said that expectations are disappointments and resentments in the making. My alternate version of this expression is that *unexpressed expectations* are disappointments and resentments waiting to happen. Clarifying expectations reduces conflict, increases relationship satisfaction, and allows everyone to know the measures for success.

We can feel the impact of this within teams and organizations. Within organizations where expectations are clear, it feels as though the team has taken a collective exhale—freeing up capacity for the most important work. Team members can relax into their work, connecting to a sense of joy, accomplishment, and purpose, because they know what is expected. In organizations where expectations are unclear or unexpressed, there is a palpable tension underneath the surface, as if team members are continuously turning up the speed on a treadmill in an attempt to feel successful, but without making forward progress. Sometimes, what appears on the surface to be a culture-related problem or, for example, a sense of pervasive burnout across the organization, can be a symptom of unclear expectations. When team members don't know how to feel successful, they may channel these frustrations in other ways or continue to work harder at the wrong thing.

HINT

BURNOUT CAN BE A SYMPTOM OF
UNCLEAR EXPECTATIONS AND WORKING
HARDER AT THE WRONG THING.

We can proactively look for opportunities to clarify expectations.[20] Examples include:

- Creating an agenda for the meeting instead of winging it
- Clarifying whether we need an hour or if twenty minutes would be plenty
- Asking up front—what are you expecting from me, and what am I expecting from you?
- Asking our client, "What are your key business drivers?"
- Asking our team members, colleagues, and even our clients, "How can I be easier to work with?"
- Clarifying that yes, this is a business lunch, and no, this is not a date
- Asking, "What would you like from me?" or "How can I best support you?" rather than jumping in immediately with advice
- Talking through how to deal with challenging situations in advance, rather than waiting until we are in a bind
- Looking for energy leaks in our work or our lives and considering what we can do to close them or seal them. These might include unfinished conversations, open-ended invitations, or relationships that we have let fade that we could consciously complete.
- Asking team members, "Would you like me to do something with this feedback? Or are you just hoping to vent?"

Life is messy, and humans are complicated, which means that we will experience ambiguity. This is part of being human. That said, there are small but impactful things we can do to create more clarity—and therefore more ease—for all involved along the way.

EXPLORE

SQUISHY EXPECTATIONS	CLEAR EXPECTATIONS
We wing it in our relationships.	We consciously design our relationships.
We have energy leaks in our lives, whether with relationships, lingering commitments, or open invitations.	We work to consciously close energy leaks in our lives, which could mean giving an answer one way or the other, clarifying commitments, or declining invitations.
We experience tension because of misaligned expectations.	We talk through expectations in advance, to surface any areas of misalignment early in the process.
We are working harder at the wrong things.	We are working smarter at the right things.

REFLECT

1. What is one small step that I could take to create more clarity in my work, with my team, or in my life?

2. How have I clearly articulated expectations with my team?

3. What opportunities exist within my personal life to create more clarity around expectations?

4. What energy leaks exist in my work or my life—and what could it look like to close them?

5. What are the things within my work or life that I need to consciously complete?

BE CURIOUS:

LEAD BY LISTENING
FOR CLUES

LEAP FROM THE TRAPEZE: CURIOSITY VERSUS CERTAINTY

We're mental misers: we often prefer the ease of hanging on to old views over the difficulty of grappling with new ones.

—Adam Grant, *Think Again*

"I don't know," she said.

"What do I like? I don't know.

"What are my hobbies? I don't know.

"What am I passionate about right now? I don't know."

We were catching up over coffee, and Beth was explaining the ways in which her perspectives had shifted since becoming a mother fourteen months ago. "It has caused me to question *everything*," she said. "It's as if I suddenly have no idea how to answer these questions that were previously so clear and simple. I'm reexamining it all." She shared this with a spirit of tenderness and compassion toward herself. It was a beautiful example of falling in love with the space in between.

We live in a society that often values confidence over competence; certainty over curiosity; and talking over listening. We watch politicians yell at each other from behind their podiums, slinging pre-rehearsed soundbites rather than asking substantive questions or having respectful conversations. In the most egregious examples, there has been so little listening that the debate hosts implemented a mute feature, after all other attempts at encouraging listening and civilized dialogue failed. At work, team members are praised for speaking up and showing confidence in meetings, while others are coached on the need to speak up more or be more visible.

Through their research on confidence in the workplace, which was published in the article "The Confidence Gap" and later the book, *The Confidence Code*,[1] Katty Kay and Claire Shipman found that in the workplace, confidence is valued as much as, or even more than, competence. This can be an issue for those who are naturally less confident, who are more introverted, or who are soft spoken. Add to this the Dunning Kruger Effect[2]—the idea that people with a low ability at a task tend to overestimate their abilities—and we have some problems.

We can see the issue of false confidence play out in management and leadership as well. One study in Norway revealed that 80 percent of managers said that "creating commitment and motivation is a field they have mastered," while under half of employees say that their bosses "deliver on important factors that contribute to engagement."[3]

As leaders, we can model a different way of being by embracing the space in between—between black and white, right and wrong, good and bad. We can be open to the nuance and accepting of shades of gray. By being curious and open, we allow ourselves to be informed by the world around us—being open to new information, new inputs, new ideas, and new advances in technology that may inform our thinking or our worldview. Rather than clinging to certainty, our opportunity invite curiosity. Danaan Parry talks about a related idea in "The Parable of the Trapeze,"[4] as he describes life as a series of trapeze swings, "either hanging on to a trapeze bar swinging along or, for a few moments in my life, I'm hurtling across space in between trapeze bars." Our opportunity is to embrace the space in between and to loosen our grip on the trapeze bar that we are holding if it is no longer serving us, or the situation at hand.

Humans are naturally curious beings. We see this innate trait in children. Many children frequently ask questions; they have a seemingly insatiable desire to understand the way things work, why things are the way they are, and how the world functions as it does. As we get older, however, we are conditioned to believe that knowing answers is preferable to asking questions. We are praised for raising our hands and getting perfect scores on tests. We memorize facts and terminology; we get into colleges and competitive companies by getting things right.

This commitment to certainty, while helpful for tests and rote memorization and specific scenarios, can diminish our effectiveness as leaders. We live in a rapidly changing world. The answers that lead us to today are likely not the same answers that will lead us toward tomorrow. As leaders working to create Expansive Impact, we can practice letting go of certainty and opening ourselves to curiosity. We want to avoid becoming, as Adam Grant explores in his book *Think Again*, experts in a world that no longer exists.

So how do we do this? We can start by being present, open, curious, and engaged—present to the moment that is before us; open to the sights and sounds and inputs and clues; curious about what is, what could be, and what is possible; and engaged with our current reality. Rather than clinging tightly to what we think we know, we can hold our ideas loosely and allow them to be informed by the wealth of information that surrounds us every day. Rather than trying to look good and get it right, we can be curious about what is and what could be.

Can you imagine what a different world we might live in if, rather than politicians spewing their soundbites at each other, they instead sat down and had a conversation from a place of genuine curiosity? A world where we can feel confident and clear about the things that matter most, while also being curious about what could be and about the perspectives and points of view that are different than our own? A world where disparaging opinion pieces published via mainstream media were replaced by round-table discussions, and where Twitter arguments were replaced by compassionate discussions over dinner? I dream about this type of world and hope that one day we will get there. In the meantime, we can work to create this type of world within our own spheres—with our families, our friends, our team members, our clients, and our colleagues.

EXPLORE

CERTAINTY	CURIOSITY
This is how it is.	What could be?
Black and white	Shades of gray and multicolor
Gripping tightly to the trapeze bar	Embracing trapeze moments
My perspectives are formed based on the constraints of my own worldview.	I allow my perspective to be informed by new data, information, and ideas that may be different from my own.

REFLECT

1. How is my need for certainty getting in my way?

2. What could it look like to be clear and grounded in what feels true, while being open and curious to what could be?

3. How is a sense of certainty getting in the way of innovation or creativity within my team or organization?

4. What could it look like to allow myself to be surprised and delighted by new information?

5. In what areas might my thinking be wrong? How can I allow it to be informed by new information and new data?

UNDERSTANDING
AND AGREEMENT:
THEY AREN'T THE SAME

When we lead with fear and anger, we eventually become the very aggressors we are fighting against. We become what we despise.

—Zainab Salbi, *Freedom Is an Inside Job*

ave you ever driven down the street, seen a yard sign for a political candidate that you don't support, and formed an immediate judgment about the person who lives in the house? If so, you aren't alone. It is easy to make a split-second decision about whether we agree with someone on a topic and decide that we either accept and understand this person or that we don't. This way of thinking—basing understanding and acceptance on whether we agree—has led to significant chasms in our world. You may also think of an example within your workplace—a person with whom you disagree on a topic or an issue, and as a result, whom you have a hard time understanding and accepting.

In our society, we see the following scenario play out:

- Do I agree with this person?
- If yes, I understand and accept them.
- If not, I neither understand nor accept them—and in fact, I feel disdain, disgust, or even hatred toward them.

This way of thinking has become further and further amplified. It seems that even the most arcane topics have become fuel for division and polarization. Rather than engaging in dialogue, we spew vitriol online; rather than sharing our feedback, we leave a scathing review; rather than getting curious, we cancel someone.

This way of operating is creating anything but forward progress and positive impact and is pushing us further away from each other. I have witnessed countless friendships and even sibling relationships dissolved due to a disagreement over a single political, societal, or policy-related issue. Years and even decades of shared history, camaraderie, friendship, and love were dismissed in an instant over a simple disagreement about a single topic. We must ask ourselves:

- Is this the price we are willing to pay for agreement?
- Must we agree at all costs?
- What will matter most on our deathbeds—the relationships we have, or the fact that we clung to the notion of being right?
- What if there is beauty and freedom to be found in the fact that we don't all have to agree?

HINT

UNDERSTANDING AND AGREEMENT
ARE NOT THE SAME THING.

Our opportunity as leaders is not to work toward 100 percent agreement or consensus. Rather, our opportunity is to cultivate understanding. We can do this by embracing a spirit of curiosity, asking questions, and coming from a place of acceptance, rather than a place of seeking agreement.

This means flipping a common way of operating.

Rather than starting with "Do we agree or disagree?" we can start from a place of humility, and openness. From here, we can work to cultivate understanding through curiosity and dialogue. And finally, we may agree or disagree; at this point, whether we agree or not doesn't really matter. What matters is that we've been open to having a conversation, that we've invited dialogue, and that we have worked to stretch our perspective in new and expanded ways.

Here, it is important to mention that this work feels more crucial than ever. I have never witnessed more examples of this concept going awry than I have during the years that I spent writing this book. The number of times that I heard insults and hateful comments lobbed out into the open, targeting anyone who held opinions or beliefs deemed to be wrong, without any effort to understand an opposing point of view was astounding and, frankly heartbreaking. I heard these comments even from leaders who are typically compassionate, even from people who meditate, even from those who typically embrace nuance, and even from those who do a lot of personal development work. The more divided our society has become, the more critical it is that we, as leaders, are able to embrace the paradox as an alternative to polarization; to hold space for multiple perspectives and points of view; and to take a stand against disdain and hatred toward those who are different or who disagree. The change toward a more conscious and compassionate world begins with us.

Disagreeing with someone does not mean that they are wrong, and that we are right. It simply means that we disagree.

EXPLORE

CLINGING TO AGREEMENT	CULTIVATING UNDERSTANDING
We start from a place of "Do we agree?"	We start from a place of acceptance.
We find it difficult to understand or accept those who have a different view than we do.	We work to understand and accept those who have a different view than we do.
We surround ourselves with others who think like us, act like us, and have similar points of view.	We surround ourselves with a diverse group of people who have varying viewpoints, perspectives, and life experiences.
Agreement comes first.	Acceptance comes first.

REFLECT

1. What could it look like to cultivate understanding from a place of acceptance?

2. What could it look like to let go of the need to agree—and allow myself to be curious and open?

3. In what ways am I intentionally or unintentionally be creating communities or circles around myself that are based in agreement rather than curiosity or dialogue?

4. Where would I benefit from agreeing to disagree?

5. Where in my life am I placing judgments upon someone who I disagree with, rather than seeking to understand?

HEAR THE MUSIC
OF LIFE THROUGH
EXPANSIVE LISTENING

Silence is like a cradle holding our endeavors and our will; a silent
spaciousness sustains us in our work and at the same time connects us
to larger worlds that, in the busyness of our daily struggle to achieve,
we have not yet investigated. Silence is the soul's break for freedom.

—David Whyte

Expansive listening is an opportunity to listen in a bigger way. Commonly when we are listening, we are listening to respond, we are listening to react, we are solving a problem in our head, or we are waiting to speak.

Expansive listening allows us to hear what is being said and absorb what we're hearing. We can think of this as not only listening to the words that are being said, but also to everything that comes along with the words, including emotions, subtle clues, gestures, and an overall feeling of connection.

We can practice this when we are in conversation with others and when we are out in the world. The late Pauline Oliveros called this deep listening.[5] In her TED Talk entitled "The Difference between Hearing and Listening," Pauline, a musician, tells the story of playing fully improvised music in a cistern. "In order to play in a cistern environment, we had to learn to listen in a new way. We had no plan, no written score, and had no discussion beforehand. We simply improvised, played, and learned that the cistern was playing with us. We had to respect the sound that was coming back to us from the cistern walls and include it in our musical sensibilities. All of this was unspoken and simply experienced by the three of us."

We can think of the world around us as our own cistern. Each time that we play our metaphorical music, whether while having a conversation, giving a talk, or leading a meeting, our environment is speaking back to us. Our opportunity is to listen.

Even in a virtual environment, via video conference, or when everyone has their cameras turned off and it seems like we aren't getting any input from participants, we are always getting feedback from both the people around us and from our environment. Our opportunity as leaders is to pay attention, notice it, and consciously respond.

We can practice expansive listening in four ways:

- Within ourselves
- With others
- Within teams and groups
- Within the world around us

Expansive Listening within Ourselves

Expansive listening within ourselves is a way to remain connected to our strong and steady center, no matter what is happening around us. This does not mean that we must be right or certain, but it means staying grounded and present, so that we can consciously respond to the moment before us. It allows us to take in new information in a thoughtful, intentional, and curious way. It means checking in to consider, "What feels true for me right now?" and "Am I living in my own truth and integrity?" We can think of this as listening to our intuition, our inner wisdom, our inner truth, and our higher self. When we practice expansive listening within ourselves, it means that we do not abandon ourselves during conversations or exchanges. We practice kindness and friendship toward ourselves.

Expansive Listening with Others

Expansive listening with others involves listening from a place of openness and curiosity to what another person is saying—without rehearsing what we are going to say in our head, waiting to speak, judging, assuming, or projecting. We are truly *hearing* what the other person is saying—without making up our own stories about their words. Listening in this way doesn't necessarily mean that we *agree* with what the other person is saying. Understanding is not the same as agreeing, as we explored previously. It means that we are open to hearing what other people have to say. When we listen in this way, we take steps toward greater understanding—and, in some cases, even healing.

Expansive Listening within Teams and Groups

Expansive listening within teams and groups involves taking in all of what is happening with both the people and the energy involved. If we are leading a virtual meeting, we can think of this as paying attention not only to the person who is talking, but to the *other* little squares on the screen as well—the equivalent to listening to everyone in the room, in equal measure.

During an in-person meeting, this may involve reading the room, picking up on body language, and checking in if the room suddenly becomes quiet. It could mean naming the elephant in the room so that the group can work with it, instead of working around it. We can suggest a quick break if the energy in the room is dragging. Expansive listening involves listening to all of what is happening and using this information in a conscious and intentional way.

Expansive Listening within the World around Us

Finally, expansive listening within the world around us involves being open to clues from our surroundings. This could mean taking clues from nature, from an opportunity that presents itself, or from a run-in with a friend we haven't seen in a decade. In daily life, this can be something as simple as paying attention to the parking spot that becomes open just as we are pulling into the lot and seizing the opportunity. On a conference call, this may mean acknowledging, rather than ignoring, the clap of thunder in the background. This might also mean paying attention when the stars aren't aligning, and instead of pushing harder, pausing to consider what needs to shift and if we are hard at work...on the wrong thing.

We can think of listening to the world around us as swimming with the current, rather than against it—a concept we will explore later in the book. When employing this method of listening, we are open to the clues and information that surround us in any given moment, and we use these clues to inform our leadership and our actions. To use Pauline's example from earlier, listening within the world around us means acknowledging that the metaphorical cistern is always echoing back to us. Our opportunity is to listen.

Expanding Our Typical Ways of Listening

Have you ever been talking with someone, when all of a sudden, a wave of emotion came over you? Perhaps you said, out loud or to yourself, "Wow, I'm not sure where that came from." This may have happened in a therapy session, a coaching session, or while talking with a beloved or a close friend. Perhaps it happened talking with an acquaintance or someone you'd just met. Maybe it happened at the end of a yoga class or on a walk with a colleague. I witness this when I'm sitting in circles with others. Chances are, if this has happened to you, you received the gift of expansive listening.

Being listened to can be a powerful and even emotional experience, partly because it can feel so rare. Can you imagine the healing that could happen in our world through more expansive listening?

Creating Expansive Impact requires expansive listening. It involves what Stephen Covey famously coined as seeking first to understand. Expansive listening involves being in relationship with both the people and the world around us and listening openly, and being mindful of how we might unintentionally be coloring what we hear with our own opinions, judgments, or triggers (easier said than done, of course!). It involves listening to hear and to feel. It involves listening to take in information from an open and curious place.

Here are a few ways to do so.

- During conversations, we can practice getting *over there* with the other person, if we find that we are *over here* in our own stuff (our thoughts, our stories, our judgments, our responses that we are rehearsing in our own heads).
- We can work on a skill that, in the coaching world, we call self-management. This means resisting our burning desire to jump in with opinions, thoughts, and advice and instead, being curious and asking questions. Visually, I like to think of this as sitting on our hands, but in a grounded and open way. This does not mean that we abandon ourselves or our inner knowing or intuition; rather, it means that we refrain from putting everything through the lens of our own "stuff" so that we can be open and receptive to what the other person is sharing.
- We can imagine the sphere of what we can hear in a visual way. We can picture it getting bigger and bigger—creating a situation in which we can hear not only our own inner voice and dialogue but also what the other person is saying, what the other person is feeling, and the clues that exist in our surroundings and our environment.
- We can revisit the present moment. Typically, if we stop listening, it is because we have drifted off to the past or to the future. When this happens, we can notice it, and then come back to the moment that is unfolding before us.

HINT

EXPANSIVE LISTENING INVOLVES
LISTENING IN A BIGGER WAY.

John and Julie Gottman, the researchers and clinical psychologists you met earlier, have studied marriage and relationship health over the course of forty years, by studying more than three thousand couples. One of the practices that they talk about is turning toward, which is the idea that when one partner makes a bid for attention (a gesture, a comment, a joke, a request for advice or help), the other partner turns toward the person who made the bid, versus turning away. The research has found that missing a bid is more devastating than rejecting a bid—basically that if our partner tries to reach out for connection or attention and we miss it completely, that it is much more hurtful than if our partner would have said, "It's not a good time; can we talk in five minutes?"

This dynamic plays out in professional settings as well. Team members feel hurt, rejected, and devalued when they feel that their leaders have missed their bids. We can go back to the story of Heidi and Bob from the first section of the book. Remember their moments of morning disconnection? In short, this was a decades-long disconnection that formed after Heidi continually tried to make bids for Bob's attention, and Bob continually missed them.*

Turning toward our team members is an act of connection, an act of compassion, and an act of respect and curiosity. Practically speaking, turning toward also allows us to get to know our team members better and to find out things we wouldn't otherwise know—about them, about their projects, about our shared clients—and to help our team members feel valued, appreciated, and seen.

Most of us want to feel seen, valued, and appreciated. This means we need to show up and to listen to each other with an open heart and mind. We need to *turn toward*.

---

* Here, it is important to make a note of personal responsibility: Heidi could have spoken up in service of her desires or told Bob more clearly that she wanted to connect in the mornings before the workday. But she didn't, and as a result, we saw the product of years-long culture and communication issues, rooted in a pattern of not turning toward.

Listening to Our Intuition and Inner Truth versus Our Stories and Assumptions

It is worth noting that when we are practicing expansive listening, we are still listening to ourselves and to our own intuition and inner truth. As we saw previously, expansive listening includes listening to ourselves, listening to others, listening within groups and teams, and listening to the world around us.

Sometimes it can be difficult to discern our intuition from our stories, judgments, fears, or assumptions. A question I receive from clients is "How can I tell if this is my intuition, or if this is anxiety? How can I tell if this is my own inner knowing, or if this is fear?"

These are excellent questions that are not always easy to answer. As a general guideline (knowing that there is, of course, nuance with each individual situation), our intuition is present focused, where fear is focused on the past or future. Our intuition may have an underlying feeling of clarity, whereas fear or the voice of the saboteur has an energy that is less settled. Our intuition is connected to our highest good, as if it's saying, "This is what is best for you." Our saboteurs are often *afraid* of what is best for us, because in order to create what's best, we may need to let go of what is known, steady, and safe. Our saboteurs cause us to suffer twice or three times by replaying the past and worrying about the future, rather than being in the moment. We can work to discern the voice of our intuition from the voice of our saboteur by continually coming back to the question of "Is it true?"

Where in our lives are we attempting to override our intuition and our inner knowing with our logical minds? While it is helpful to consider both intuition and logic, I've observed that most of us are better at honoring our logical minds than we are at honoring our intuition.

HINT

INTUITION IS OFTEN PRESENT-FOCUSED.
ASSUMPTIONS, DOUBTS, AND STORIES ARE
OFTEN PAST- OR FUTURE-FOCUSED.

In *The Gift of Fear,* Gavin DeBecker[6] shares several terrifying stories about the impact on people who have overridden their intuition and used their logical minds to convince themselves that their intuition wasn't valid—situations in which a stranger was just a little *too friendly,* or a neighbor was just a little *too insistent* on helping to carry the groceries. Each story featured individuals who had a strong, intuitive sense that something wasn't right, but they overrode their intuition because they wanted to be nice, be neighborly, or not risk being dramatic. In short, none of these situations ended well. Our intuition is powerful; as leaders, our opportunity is to tune in and listen.

This is yet another call for both/and: to honor *both* the gifts of our logical minds *and* our inner knowing and intuition. This means tuning into our own inner truth, while also being open to the world around us.

It can be helpful to create a few simple practices that allow us to connect to our own intuition and our own inner knowing. For some, this involves meditation. For others, this involves morning exercise, in order to be more present and focused for the rest of the day. For many clients, it is a quick pause before replying to an email or a request.

EXPLORE

HEARING	EXPANSIVE LISTENING
Waiting to speak or respond	Seeking first to understand
Predicting what the other person is going to say	Allowing ourselves to be open and curious to what the other person is saying
Staying "over here" in our own stuff—our stories, experiences, or examples	Getting "over there" with the other person
Moving through the world in a way that is closed off to the data and information around us	Moving through the world in a way that is open and receptive to the data and information around us

REFLECT

1. What is my natural way of listening?

2. What could it look like to practice expansive listening within my leadership and my life?

3. Who in my life do I find challenging to listen to? How could I apply the practice of expansive listening with this person?

4. Where might my intellect be getting in the way of my ability to practice expansive listening?

5. Where am I getting hooked by disagreement or judgment? What could it look like to listen from a place of acceptance and seeking to understand?

ASK BETTER QUESTIONS TO
GET BETTER INFORMATION

---

*I think, at a child's birth, if a mother could ask a fairy godmother to
endow it with the most useful gift, that gift would be curiosity.*

—Eleanor Roosevelt

Sometimes, during a Zing Collaborative Leadership experience,
we undertake an exercise in which participants have just one
minute to ask each other curiosity-based questions. No matter
how long the team members have been working together, or
how well they know each other, or how many projects they've worked
on together, they have a consistent result: during this single minute, they
learn something new about each other.

After completing this exercise with one of his team members, Jose, a
foreman for a commercial and industrial roofing company, exclaimed,
"I've known this guy for twenty-five years, and he's like a brother to me,
but I didn't know any of this stuff until today!"

In another example from a regional construction company, Zeke, a director, reported back during our monthly gathering, "I tried this with my wife, and holy crap, I feel like it just improved my marriage overnight!"

This is the power of asking questions from a place of curiosity. If we want to get better information, we need to ask better questions. And if we want to increase our capacity to lead, to build relationships, deepen our understanding, and expand our perspective, we can do so by asking better questions.

Typically, better questions, which we will call Curiosity-Based Questions, have two specific qualities: they are open ended, and they begin with either "what" or "how." "What" or "how" questions open new possibilities; they explore what could be, and they typically lead to more expansive answers than closed ended or "why" questions. Additionally, unlike "why" questions, they create an environment that feels safe, open, and curious—rather than putting others on the defensive.[7]

HINT

CURIOSITY-BASED QUESTIONS ARE OPEN-
ENDED AND BEGIN WITH "WHAT" OR "HOW."

As leaders, we will find ourselves living and leading in the liminal phase—the place in between. We lead our teams from the old toward the new. We lead our team members from their time as a new professional toward their first promotion. We lead our colleagues from the difficult questions toward the possible paths forward. Asking curiosity-based questions allows us to dance with the unknown and be in relationship with the in-between. They allow us to live, and even thrive, in the questions rather than needing to rush toward the answers.

Leaning into the questions allows us to be informed by the world around us. It opens us up to the possibility of changing our minds when we have new information, new perspectives, or a broader picture than we had before. Quite simply, stepping forward into the questions allows us to be more inclusive, more expansive, and more adaptable leaders.

We can practice living into the questions in everyday life by challenging ourselves to think beyond what we think we know. We can try on questions such as[9]:

- What could be?
- What's possible?
- What might I be missing?
- What new information is available to me?
- What might others be carrying in their metaphorical backpacks that I'm not aware of?

In our relationships with friends, family members, and partners, rather than assuming we know what they're thinking or feeling or why they're doing what they're doing, we can make an effort to find out by asking questions such as:

- How are you doing today?
- What is currently giving you energy?
- How do you like to spend your time?
- What are you feeling excited about these days?
- What's a current challenge that you're facing?
- How has your thinking evolved on this topic over the years?
- What's a new curiosity or interest that you have lately?

- What is something that's currently feeling meaningful to you?

And out in the world—and related to hot topics (especially those that can be polarizing)—we can consider questions such as:

- How might my perspective on this topic be limited?
- What information am I missing?
- What is the 1 percent truth in the other point of view or the other person's perspective?
- How could I expand my knowledge or my perspective on this topic?
- How might others be seeing this differently than the way I'm seeing it?
- Where am I living, working, or communicating within an echo chamber—meaning that I'm missing out on important, alternate points of view?
- How might I unintentionally be *contributing to* an echo chamber?
- Where am I slapping labels on other people and making judgments as a result?
- How might other people's values be different than my own—leading people to different conclusions or decisions?

Be Mindful of Advice Masked as a Question

Asking curiosity-based questions invites us to let go of our natural tendency to give advice masked as a question. Advice masked as a question sounds like...

- *Have you thought about...*
- *Have you considered...*
- *Why don't you try...*
- *What about doing...*

Do you see how it's easy to sneak in advice under this convincing cloak of a question? These questions aren't bad, necessarily, but they can be limiting, especially in situations where the other person doesn't actually *want* our advice. If we aren't sure, we can ask, "Would you like me to just listen, or would you like my advice?"

Do you have a favorite framework that you use for advice masked as questions? If so, without judgment, I invite you to notice.

Then, you can begin to shift from advice masked as a question toward asking open-ended, curiosity-based questions that may lead to new possibilities and even greater solutions.

If you catch yourself offering advice masked as a question when it isn't desired, you can pause, take a breath, and consider rephrasing it as a curiosity-based question. This means setting aside our burning desire to tell the other person what they should do and instead, allowing ourselves to be genuinely curious about what is present and what is possible.

Curiosity-based questions are a helpful tool in our toolbox. At the end of the day, people want to feel valued, seen, and appreciated as human beings. Taking the time to ask a question and then listen to the response is one way to create this sense of appreciation.

My friend Suzanne has one of the happiest relationships that I've observed from afar. When I asked her about her secret sauce, she said, "Sarah, the trick is that we stay infinitely curious about each other. We never assume that we know everything about each other, even though we've been together for many years now. We keep asking questions, and we continue to be curious day after day. This keeps the spark alive and keeps us continually learning and growing together."

EXPLORE

BEING CERTAIN AND GIVING ADVICE	ASKING AND BEING CURIOUS
Closed-ended	Open-ended
We ask why.	We ask "what" or "how."
We give advice.	We ask questions.
We give advice masked as a question.	We ask a question from a place of curiosity.

REFLECT

1. What relationships in my life would benefit from more curiosity-based questions?

2. How can I use curiosity-based questions to open new possibilities with my team members and colleagues?

3. How might I unintentionally be putting people on the defensive by asking "why" questions?

4. How can I let go of what I think I know, in order to be delighted and surprised by what I find out?

5. How can I allow myself to be surprised and delighted by the person and the moment in front of me?

TAKE A COACH
APPROACH

When you build a coaching habit, you can more easily break
out of three vicious circles that plague our workplaces: creating
overdependence, getting overwhelmed and becoming disconnected.
— Michael Bungay Stanier

A coaching-based approach is one in which we use the power of expansive listening and curiosity-based questions, in service of greater outcomes. With this approach, we don't need to know all the answers. We don't need to focus on looking good or getting it right. Rather, we can be open, we can listen expansively, and we can ask curiosity-based questions to help our team members, colleagues, and loved ones uncover the answers that are within them.

Taking a coaching-based approach allows us to do what Ken Blanchard described in his book *The One Minute Manager Meets the Monkey* as giving back the monkey.[10] As managers and leaders, we may find ourselves taking on other people's metaphorical monkeys—our team members' problems, questions, issues, ideas, suggestions, and complaints. This means that at the end of the day, we have sixty-two things to follow up on—none of which are from our own to-do list!

When we step into a coaching-based approach, rather than taking these things on *from* our team members, we give them back—along with support, guidance, and curiosity-based questions that will help our team members move forward. In addition to keeping the monkeys off our shoulders, so to speak, this is a much more empowering and growth-oriented approach for our team members. We are trusting our team members to uncover the answers that they already have within them; we are then providing encouragement and guidance along the way.

If we were to bottom-line this coaching-based approach, it would include:

- SET THE AGENDA—ask, "What is the goal for this conversation?"
- ASK CURIOSITY-BASED QUESTIONS—ask "what" or "how" questions to uncover new information and new possibilities about the topic.
- PRACTICE EXPANSIVE LISTENING—use what you learn and discover to inform the questions that you ask next.
- ACTION AND AGREEMENTS—after exploring the topic through a mix of curiosity-based questions and expansive listening, empower your team member to move the topic or action forward in some way that feels meaningful.[11]

Being a good coach and a good leader means asking good questions. It means caring about the person in front of you. It means coming from a place of curiosity, instead of assuming that we know the answers or placing blame. It means being open, present, and curious.

Many of my clients work in industries and roles where they're accustomed to figuring things out and needing to know all of the answers—for the technology solution, on the jobsite, or to determine the new employee compensation plan. As a result, bringing a coaching-based approach to their leadership can feel unnatural, unusual, and downright painful at times. If you relate to this, you're not alone.

But the promising thing about bringing a coaching-based approach to our leadership is that ultimately, it makes our job easier. Rather than needing to know all the answers, we can ask curiosity-based questions, empower our team members to uncover the answers that live within them, and also uncover new possibilities that we otherwise wouldn't have.

One of the reasons that we've spent so much time in this book talking about being present and clearing out our assumptions and stories is so that we can show up fully with those around us. We have this opportunity each time we meet with our team members.

If we come in distracted, fired up about an issue, or spinning stories in our heads, we are not present—and we are not going to be effective in our role as coaches. We need to clear out the things that get in the way of our ability to be fully present with the person across from us—or the person whose face appears on the screen before us. It is from this place of presence that we can be an effective coach and leader.

Let's talk in depth about these steps, to create a structure that you can use each time you coach your team members or colleagues—whether formally or informally.

Set the Agenda

This first step involves clarifying the agenda: What will you talk about during your 1:1 meeting or coaching session? Ideally, this agenda is set by, or in collaboration with, your team member or the person you're coaching. In a typical team member/manager relationship, both people contribute to the agenda; for maximum success, it can be helpful to clarify these topics ahead of time.

Important note: effective 1:1 meetings and effective coaching sessions are not status update meetings. In fact, one possible outcome of this book could be that you eliminate status update meetings altogether, because upon reviewing the core purpose of your meetings and improving the quality of your conversations, you decide that they're no longer needed.

We can clarify our agendas by asking the following questions:

- What are the most important things we should talk about today?
- What are our top three topics for this time together?

We can also clarify what success looks like for this conversation:

- What will success look like for today's 1:1?
- What would you most like to get from this time together?
- How can I be most helpful to you today?
- What would you like to walk away with?

Ask Curiosity-Based Questions

After setting the agenda, you, with your coaching hat on, have an opportunity to get curious and ask questions. This means putting into practice everything we've talked about so far in this section of this book—most notably, asking open-ended questions that begin with "what" or "how."

To kick off the coaching session, you might ask questions about the current state, such as:

- What's the current state of this topic?
- How are things going?

- What specifically would you like to dig into, related to this topic?
- What's the high-level, current-state synopsis?

From here, we can dig in based on what is happening and what is needed from the conversation, whether that's solving a challenge, uncovering possibilities, clarifying steps forward, or getting something unstuck.

In short, we want to ask concise, open-ended questions that begin with "what" or "how," related to our team member's topic.[12]

Practice Expansive Listening

A critical supplement to asking questions is listening. If we listen fully to what our team members and colleagues are telling us, we will naturally uncover additional questions to ask. Here, you may employ the skill of Expansive Listening.

Action and Agreements

Finally, after we have clarified our topic, asked questions, and listened, we can begin to identify next steps and actions. During this final step, it is helpful to be very specific about what will happen next and who is responsible for moving the process forward. During this section, helpful questions include:

- What are the next steps?
- Who will do what, by when?
- What is your definition of done?
- What is my definition of done?
- Where might we have discrepancies between our two definitions of done? How can we resolve them now versus later?
- How do we want to check in?
- What type of accountability works best for you?

If we follow this structure, we will likely have a productive coaching conversation. Our goal as leaders, managers, and coaches is to continue to practice these steps until they begin to feel natural and instinctive.

As Michael Bungay Stanier writes in *The Coaching Habit*, "Building a coaching habit is about staying curious a little longer and rushing to advice-giving a little more slowly."[13] I would agree with his assessment, as well as his idea that becoming a good coach is, indeed, a habit that we can build and practice over time.

Coaching the Person versus Coaching Their Work

There is a difference between coaching, managing, and leading the whole human being and coaching the topics, projects, and details of what that human being is working on. It is helpful to know the distinction.

As leaders and managers, especially if we are ultimately responsible for the success of these topics/projects/details, it can be tempting to jump straight to status updates and project reports.

We are leading, managing, and coaching *humans*, not just the things that they are working on. I believe one of the most unfortunate terms ever created is Human Resources. Humans are far more than resources, and as leaders we need to act accordingly.[14]

A few simple ways to make sure we are coaching the person and not just the topic:

- Asking, "How are you?" and meaning it.
- When talking about topics, projects, and details, asking, "What is important about this to you?"
- Carving out time during each 1:1—even if only for a few minutes— to talk about your team member, how things are going, and any important developments happening in work or life.

As we are working to embrace a coaching-based approach, we can check in with ourselves to consider the following questions:

- In meetings with team members, am I talking more or listening more? Am I establishing a comfortable balance? What could it look like to shift toward listening more and talking less, if this helps to create a better balance?
- Do I typically ask or tell? What could it look like to shift toward asking more questions, if my natural style is to give advice?
- What could it look like to empower my team members to find the answers and the solutions within *themselves*?
- How can I strike a balance between coaching and managing *the work* and coaching and managing *the person*? Am I making time for both during our conversations?

EXPLORE

TELLING	COACHING
Tasks, projects, deliverables, timelines	The human *behind* the tasks, projects, deliverables, timelines
Telling our team members what to do	Asking our team members what they think they should do
Taking on tasks, issues, and questions from our team members	Empowering our team members to answer their own questions by finding the answers that live within them
We do most of the talking; our team members do most of the listening.	We do most of the listening; our team members do most of the talking.

REFLECT

1. What could it look like to bring a coaching-based approach to my meetings with my team members?

2. What structures do I have in place for coaching conversations with my team members? If they don't exist, how could I create them?

3. As a leader, how can I strike a balance between offering suggestions or guidance and asking questions?

4. What could it look like to set up a coaching-based agenda with my colleagues or team members?

5. What gets in the way of effective coaching? How can I examine this so that I can show up more effectively with my team members?

THE EAGLE AND
THE SEAGULL

The bugle blast of evaluation can drown out the quieter
melodies of coaching and appreciation.

—Douglas Stone and Sheila Heen

---

t's 4:00 p.m. on a Friday. Peggy has just one item remaining on her
to-do list, which is to check in with Tom about yesterday's presentation. While the presentation went well overall, there are a few things
that need to be addressed by next week. Peggy swings by Tom's office,
where he is packing up for the day.

"Tom, you did a great job on yesterday's presentation. However, a few
quick things: we didn't account for the needs of the East Coast market,
we missed a key piece of feedback from our supply chain lead, and there
was an error on the third slide. Oh, and we need to create a condensed
version of the presentation for our executive team. They'd like to see
it on Monday. No big deal—just thirty minutes with the full exec suite.
The meeting is scheduled for 9:00 a.m. Would you mind taking care of

those things whenever you have a chance? Thanks so much! Have a great weekend!"

Peggy breezes down the hall, heads toward the door, and unlocks her car from afar. The "ding, ding" of the unlocking car signals the start of the weekend. Peggy feels free and accomplished, excited that she crossed off that final item on the list. She cranks up the volume on her favorite playlist and cruises toward the weekend.

Meanwhile, Tom is in his office, standing in silence, dumbfounded, his backpack in his hand, unsure of what just happened. Can these items wait until Monday morning? He'd likely need to come in at 6:00 a.m. to get everything done before the 9:00 a.m. meeting. Or should he cancel his happy hour plans and dive back into the slide deck? Just five minutes ago, he had been ready to celebrate a successful week with three of his closest friends. Now, it doesn't feel like he has much to celebrate.

If this scenario sounds familiar in any way, you were likely involved in your own case of Seagull-ing: as either the seagull (Peggy) or the one fielding the unexpected droppings (Tom).

The Seagull Effect is when someone, typically in a leadership role or a position of power, flies by and drops something on their team members below, leaving those on the ground in a state of surprise, or even shock. Meanwhile, the seagull continues to fly overhead, feeling productive and accomplished, as Peggy did in the scenario above. Unfortunately, when we think that we are coaching our team members, providing feedback, or crossing something off the list, we are doing something that feels an awful lot like seagull-ing to those standing below. This does not help our team members to grow, and it certainly is not motivating for others. Rather, it leaves those around us holding the droppings (for example, an amorphous piece of feedback or a task that we've tossed to someone else), wondering what to do with it. Our opportunity as leaders is to not just share feedback or random to-dos, but to engage in coaching, dialogue, and conversation.

The alternative to being a seagull is being an eagle. If the seagull swoops down unexpectedly and leaves droppings in its path, the eagle soars above the clouds, taking the birds'-eye view and keeping things in perspective. The eagle sees, and remains connected to, the big picture. The eagle is responsive rather than reactive, discerning rather than distracted. In everyday life, while the seagulls are fighting on social media, the eagle is connected to its higher purpose, focused on its goals, and dropping off a home-cooked meal for its neighbor. The eagle stays connected to the things that matter most stays anchored to its grounded and steady center.

One of the most frequent complaints I hear from managers and leaders who I work with goes something like this: "I have given my team members this feedback, and still nothing has changed." I typically have two questions in return:

- Have you *coached* this person to improve in this area, or have you merely given feedback or lobbed something over the metaphorical fence?
- What might be beneath the lack of change?

We can explore both of these questions as we coach and empower our team members toward positive impact and increased effectiveness.

The next thing that we can explore is *why* our team members are not taking the steps toward positive change that we are hoping for. To do so, we can consider a few factors that might be at play.

WHY ISN'T MY TEAM MEMBER CHANGING THEIR BEHAVIOR?

CHALLENGES & CLUES

Coaching

I have given feedback, but I haven't provided coaching.

Clue: team member is open to receiving feedback, but doesn't know what to do with the feedback.

Clarity

I have provided feedback that is ambiguous or interpretive.

Clue: team member hears and receives feedback, but behaviors don't change.

Confidence

Team member is talented, but lacks confidence in their abilities.

Clues: work takes longer than expected, there are many questions along the way, team member asks questions even though they already know the answer, team member double and triple checks work even when it might not be needed.

Capacity

Team member doesn't have time to complete the work at hand.

Clues: overwhelm, misaligned prioritization, chasing unknown targets of success.

Connection

Team member feels disconnected from the greater purpose and "why."

Clues: team member feels like they are on an island; team member doesn't see the impact of their work; team member is in an internally facing role where they don't regularly see the client/external impact of the work.

Competence

Team member isn't demonstrating the skills or aptitude needed for the role.

Clues: team member is working hard but without creating visible improvements.

Often, as managers and leaders, we think we have given clear direction and helpful feedback, but something might be missing from our approach.

Our opportunity is to get curious about why the behavior might not be changing, so that we can identify root cause and shift our approach accordingly.

POSSIBLE SOLUTIONS

Curiosity & Conversation

Set up a coaching conversation.
Ask curiosity-based questions.
Talk about how to create change and
what might be in the way.
Create a plan.

Expectations & Specifics

Set expectations.
Provide clear, actionable, and behavior-based feedback.
Avoid interpretations or judgments about the behaviors.
Ask: is this feedback specific and observable?

Reflect Back Success

Pause to recognize and celebrate wins and successes.
Instead of giving the answer, ask team members, "What do you recommend?"
Reflect back instances where your team member has known the answer on their
own, made great suggestions, or known more than they'd realized.

Prioritization

Review priorities.
Discuss expectations: are priorities aligned?
Review "emotional commitments" —things that don't take up a lot of time but that
do take up a lot of mental space.

Share the Big Picture

Talk about the big picture: why does this matter?
Share the *why* along with the *what*.
Find opportunities to see the impact of the work in action—for example, site visits.
Discuss the ways in which the work ties to company-level goals and priorities.
Make big-picture company goals visible and accessible.

Training and Coaching

Consider: what coaching and training has this team member received?
Ask: are the gaps teachable or coachable?
Consider (after doing the above): is there another role in which this team member
would thrive?
Get Curious: are there any systemic or company-wide barriers at play?

We can use the matrix on the previous pages as an invitation for reflection. First, we can look in the mirror as leaders to consider, "Have I done everything possible to help to create positive change?" And then, with our team members, colleagues, and loved ones, we can use the matrix as a guide to get curious about what is going on, about what needs to be expressed that hasn't been, and about how we can work together effectively to create a positive path forward.

EXPLORE

SEAGULL-ING	EAGLE-ING
We swoop down unannounced, leaving droppings in our path.	We engage in intentional and constructive conversations.
We lob things over the fence.	We ask, "Who is the best person to own this?"
We give feedback that lacks context or actionable opportunities for change.	We practice coaching and offer specific, actionable, and constructive suggestions.
We assume that our team member doesn't want to, or can't, change.	We look in the mirror to ask ourselves if we've provided coaching, and we get curious about what is going on.
We fight fires.	We prevent fires—and when they do arise, we spot them early.
We become obsessed with the emergency of the moment.	We keep things in perspective, we focus on our own sphere of influence, and we connect to the bigger picture.

REFLECT

1. Where am I unintentionally acting as a seagull? What could it look like to shift away from this behavior?

2. In cases where my colleagues, team members, or friends/family members aren't demonstrating the positive change that I'm hoping for, which of the factors in the table might be present?

3. What could it look like to shift from Seagull-ing to Eagle-ing at work? What about in my personal life?

4. Have I accidentally been responsible for any droppings lately? What repair or clarification is needed?

5. As a leader, how can I take responsibility for the areas of confusion above?

SECTION FIVE

BE COURAGEOUS:

LEAD WITH TRUTH
FROM THE HEART

IT IS ALL CONNECTED:
THE ISSUE AND THE SYSTEM

When we try to pick out anything by itself, we find it hitched to everything else in the Universe.

—John Muir

We do not exist in isolation. We are all connected, and most of us are part of several systems. A system is any group of more than one person—a family, a team, a division, a department, a board, a workgroup, an executive team, a group of cofounders, a neighborhood, a community. Systems have their own dynamics and their own ways of functioning. As leaders, we can start to get curious about the well-being of our systems and what we can do to help them function at a higher level.

We may find ourselves in trouble when we are acting in isolation or when we forget that we are connected to something greater. Have you ever decided, "I'll just do it myself," setting aside what this means for others? Or have you ever found yourself in moments of despair, feeling the weight of the world on your shoulders, as though everything rested on you and you alone?

As leaders, we are rarely alone. There is wisdom to be found around us. Our opportunity is to tap into it.

One way that we can do this is to consider the systems of which we are a part, and to reflect upon the wisdom, information, and insight that is available to us within these systems. We can consider, in any given moment, "What is this system trying to tell me?" and "What conflict is present within this system—and what might this conflict mean?"

There is no better place to look for inspiration than in nature. Nature is one massive system, with each animal and plant and species functioning in perfect harmony with its greater context. We can throw open the windows and the doors and peer outside, to see the ways in which innovative solutions have already been created in nature.[1] We can also see the ways in which humans continue to disrupt these natural systems and rhythms by pillaging the resources of nature for our own gain.

To be in relationship with the systems around us, our opportunity is:

- First, to identify the systems of which we are a part;
- Second, to consider the well-being of these systems;
- And third, to get curious about what information or insight is present within the system.

Let's explore this together.

In the column on the left, I'll invite you to write down the various systems of which you are a part. This could include family, friends, teams, organizations, committees, work groups, volunteer organizations, or neighbors, just to name a few.

After you write these down, let's take a moment to reflect how well these systems are functioning. If you were to assess the well-being of your systems, one to ten, how would you rate them? A score of one is a highly dysfunctional or unhealthy system; a score of ten represents a highly functional and thriving system. Feel free to go with your gut and not overthink it.

Finally, we will get curious about the wisdom that is available to us within each of these systems. What wisdom exists within? What information is present right before my eyes, if I take a closer look? What conflict exists—and what is this conflict trying to tell me? Hint: there is no right or wrong answer.

SYSTEMS THAT I AM PART OF	WELL-BEING OF THE SYSTEM	AVAILABLE INFORMATION
Example: Nonprofit board	5	*We have a few loud voices that overpower the quieter voices, which means that a handful of board members never have an opportunity to share their ideas. In this way, the board is not inclusive to all voices.*

A systems check might be something that we incorporate as part of our daily, weekly, or monthly planning process. It is a way to stay connected to the systems that we're part of and the people within, to pay attention to the wisdom of the system, and to consider, "How is the well-being of my systems?" and "What can I do to positively impact it?"

EXPLORE

THE ISSUE	THE SYSTEM
We look at things in isolation.	We look at the system as a *whole*.
We work to solve the issue at hand.	We consider: How might this issue be connected to something bigger? And what can it look like to get curious about that?
We check the issue off the list.	We resolve the urgent issues while continuing to explore the bigger challenges or themes.
We resolve one thing that breaks or disrupts something else.	We consider the ripple effects of the change.
We focus on short-term impact.	We consider both short-term and long-term impact.

REFLECT

1. What systems am I part of? How is the overall well-being of each of my systems?

2. What systems need attention—and what could it look like to engage accordingly?

3. What conflict is present within my systems?

4. What data, information, or intelligence could this conflict be offering me?

5. Where am I trying to solve an issue where instead I could be solving a system-level challenge?

EMBRACE DISHARMONY

*There's no such thing as a perfect harmony with
nature. There's a comfortable level of disharmony.
There is purposefulness in this disharmony.*

—John Chester, Apricot Lane Farms

J ohn and Molly Chester own Apricot Lane Farms, which was featured on the Netflix documentary *The Biggest Little Farm*. In the documentary, the Chesters talk about their journey to restore the farm so that it is in harmony with nature. They also explore what it means to embrace and accept the different levels of disharmony with nature. On their farm, there will always be areas of tension and disharmony. The coyotes kill the chickens, but they also kill the moles; the moles kill the crops. The birds ruin the peaches, but their droppings also fertilize the soil. The dogs protect the sheep but occasionally kill a chicken. The list goes on. They realized that their job, as farmers, was not to eliminate all the areas of conflict, but rather, to embrace them, work with them, and create from them.

Conflict is not something that we have to avoid, eliminate, manage, or tidy up in a clean and perfect way. Instead, conflict is something that we can learn to embrace. Conflict is a sign that something new is struggling to emerge, shift, or change within a system. When we look at it this way, we can get curious about what the conflict is trying to tell us and what we can create from it. Danaan Parry, in his book *Warriors of the Heart*, defines conflict as "an opportunity for intimacy." Our opportunity is to lean into conflict with an open heart and mind.

One of my colleagues talks about this as dilemma territory—the fact that we are continually experiencing dilemmas, big and small, and that we don't have to resolve them all, but rather embrace them. What dilemmas exist within you in this moment? Maybe they are small (Should I eat soup or a grain bowl for lunch today? Should I wear a tie?), or large (Should I stay in my marriage? Should I step down as CEO? Should I leave my job and start my own business? Should we downsize?).

Write a few of them down here. Allow them to surface without judgment.

Now, let's do the same thing for our teams and our organization. What are the areas of tension, the areas of disharmony, or the dilemmas that exist within your team or organization? Similar to the exercise above, they might be small, or they might be large.

Now, go back to your list and consider the following: Which areas of tension are *solvable?* Which are natural and ongoing areas of disharmony? Not all conflicts are meant to be resolved. This means that as leaders, we need to work to embrace, rather than solve, the conflict that surrounds us, and from there, we can figure out how to create from it.

John and Julie Gottman, the researchers whom you met previously, offer us the idea of perpetual problems. According to their research, some problems in marriages and relationships are perpetual, which means that they are never going to be solved. Rather, they are problems that we need to acknowledge, honor, and even embrace. We need to learn to work *with* the problems, rather than trying to eliminate them altogether.

For example, most of us face at least one perpetual problem in our friendships and relationships: different views on politics or religion; one person being more emotionally oriented and the other more logically oriented; different ideas about what parenting should (or shouldn't) look like; different ideas on spending versus saving.

It can be tempting to convince the other person to come closer to our perspective or to see things our way. We want to convince others that we are right, and that they are wrong. We want our partner to become more *like us*—to adopt our approach to money, to parenting, or to conflict. As you've likely experienced if you've tried this in your own relationship, this rarely goes well.[2] We see this playing out not only in our personal lives and on our teams, but also in our society. Rather than accepting the truth that we all have different sets of values, beliefs, and opinions about politics and religion and complicated topics, we watch people become outraged at the fact that not everyone believes the same thing (*How dare they have a different opinion?!*). We can set aside our need to solve every problem and convince other people to see things our way, and instead ask ourselves if we can accept and embrace perpetual problems and then create from them.

If you work within any type of organization, you will likely encounter perpetual problems. For example, my colleague Cy works in a nonprofit organization that she describes as highly dysfunctional. She is frequently frustrated by the level of drama and by what she describes as incompetence within the leadership team. Hearing her talk through the patterns and the history, it seems as though many of these challenges are ongoing problems that do not have quick solutions. At least several them are perpetual problems. Cy's opportunity is to decide whether she can live with them or not. If she can, her opportunity is to lead through them and create from them. If she can't, her opportunity is to move on.

I have watched many passionate colleagues try to solve problems that weren't meant to be solved within their organizations. For example, in one organization I worked with, many team members passionately spearheaded projects to reduce turnover. They prepared presentations, slide decks, and eloquent descriptions of the problem and potential solutions. But the truth was, this wasn't an area of priority for senior leadership, because the senior leaders of the organization saw turnover as a perpetual problem that they preferred to work with, rather than against. In many ways, a certain level of turnover was central to how the organization functioned, as it allowed the HR team to bring in top talent from the outside. Turnover was a perpetual problem that the leaders of the organization had embraced as part of their hiring and growth strategy. This is an example of a leadership team choosing to work *with* a perpetual problem, rather than focusing on solving or eliminating it.

As leaders, we will find ourselves with a variety of perpetual problems. For example, the lead project manager from our largest client may be someone whom we find difficult to work with. Despite our efforts to catch more flies with honey than vinegar and develop a meaningful relationship with this person, we may still find this person to be uncooperative. This may be a perpetual problem that we learn to embrace rather than solve. We can do everything we can to create ease and forge ahead, but there may always be a certain level of disharmony within the relationship. We can arrive at a both/and perspective, meaning that we can do everything within our power to improve and deepen the relationship *and* accept that some level of disharmony may persist.

In many companies, we see natural areas of tension—for example, between sales, product management, and engineering. In some cases, the sales team may be more optimistic with their timelines or with their product features than the product or engineering teams, who then need to go build what was promised. We might see similar tensions between, for example, the accounting team members who are keeping an eye on the bottom line, and the talent development team members who are looking at new ways to invest in employees. And, we may see ongoing tensions between the office and the field, or between corporate headquarters and the regional plants. While team members at the corporate headquarters may enjoy the opportunity to work from home one day per week, this is not an option for team members who are running equipment at the plant.

There is a natural disharmony that exists within a start-up that was once small and scrappy but that has now taken on investment from outside firms and is growing at a rapid rate. Each day, leaders within the organization must face the natural, and sometimes difficult, question of how to maintain culture while growing at a swift pace and undergoing significant shifts to the structure of the organization.

As small business owners, freelancers, or contractors, we may experience perpetual tension between what we say yes to and our time. If we say yes to one thing, we may need to say no to something else; if we say yes to this incoming request, we need to consider the impact to our calendar and timelines for other projects. These natural tensions will likely persist, at least to a degree. Our opportunity as leaders is not to ignore, dismiss, or try to eliminate these areas of natural tension, but rather to embrace them and create from them. Balance, the ability to prioritize, and a willingness to consider all perspectives are all necessary skills to employ.

EXPLORE

MANAGING OR TIDYING UP CONFLICT	EMBRACING AND CREATING FROM CONFLICT
We try to eliminate all areas of conflict and create harmony in all situations.	We accept a natural level of disharmony and conflict; we work with it and create from it.
We try to solve all problems.	We acknowledge that some problems are perpetual problems and, therefore, don't have solutions. We learn to work with them and lead through them.
We try to convince others that our way is right, and their way is wrong.	We accept that, at the end of the day, we are likely going to have different perspectives and different points of view.
We try to tidy up all areas of conflict or disharmony; we may sweep things under the rug.	We honor and acknowledge conflict, and we create from it.

REFLECT

1. What are the perpetual problems within my primary relationships (with my partner, family, friends, colleagues, teams, or organization)?

2. What natural areas of disharmony exist within my company or organization?

3. What can it look like to embrace and work with these perpetual problems, rather than try to solve or eliminate them?

4. What are the areas of natural disharmony within my primary relationships?

5. Where am I fighting against, rather than embracing and working with, perpetual problems?

INVITE DISCOURSE
AND CREATE
PSYCHOLOGICAL SAFETY

It is impossible to resolve a conflict, or to bring a group of people to a deep level of sharing unless you have first created a psychological and physical "space" within which the work can be done.

—Danaan Parry

Craig is the head of information technology for a healthcare organization. Whenever he speaks, his entire leadership team hangs their head and avoids eye contact. There is a visible, simultaneous movement in the room, with the leaders putting their heads down at once. The members of the leadership team not only feel unsafe to verbally disagree but feel that it is risky to speak up at all.

By contrast, Hunter is the head of information technology for a digital services company. Each month, the company tackles tough topics via an all-hands meeting. Hunter welcomes feedback, input, and questions from the team—taking detailed notes and collaborating with team members to work toward solutions to their concerns. Team members take risks, share openly, and have spirited discussions. They sometimes disagree with each other—but they do so from a place of respect and a genuine desire to understand each other's perspectives. They don't let issues fester, and instead, they tackle them head on.

Hunter's team has a high level of psychological safety. Craig's team, on the other hand, does not.

Psychological safety can be defined as being able to show and employ one's self without fear of negative consequences of self-image, status, or career.[3] Over the course of two years, the team at Google conducted 200+ interviews with Googlers and looked at more than 250 attributes of 180+ active Google teams. They found that the top quality for successful teams at Google was a sense of psychological safety.[4] They defined psychological safety at Google as "being able to take risks on this team without feeling insecure or embarrassed."

Thriving organizations commonly have significant levels of disagreement. The key is that this disagreement is grounded in a foundation of respect and understanding. In other words, thriving organizations and teams have high levels of psychological safety. It is worth noting that a lack of psychological safety can sometimes appear on the surface as agreement or harmony. With an initial glance, it may look as though everyone agrees. Beneath the surface, however, there may be fear and apprehension about the impact of speaking up or disagreeing.

A high level of psychological safety is essential for high-performing teams.

During a recent leadership series for a midsized university, someone asked, "There is a high level of psychological safety on our team, but some team members don't *feel* that there is. How should I handle this?" As leaders, our opportunity is to get curious about *why* this might be the case and consider the ways in which we are unintentionally or subconsciously creating a culture or team dynamic that feels safe for some but unsafe for others.

We can consider:

- How are we building an organizational culture in which all voices can be expressed and heard?
- How are we creating an environment in which all team members feel welcomed and appreciated?
- How are we designing an environment that fosters a sense of belonging not just for some team members but for all?
- What spoken or unspoken rules, norms, patterns, or tendencies are playing out that are causing this to be the case?
- What are we doing to invite different perspectives and different points of view?

Our opportunity is to get curious, ask questions, and deepen our understanding so that we can build a culture in which all team members can thrive.

Within teams and organizations with traditional reporting structures, there will likely be an inherent power dynamic that impacts psychological safety, at least to a degree. Sometimes, during a workshop on Embracing Conflict, I invite teams to share their perceived level of psychological safety within their organizations via an anonymous poll. Those in management and leadership roles consistently rate the psychological safety of the organization higher than those in individual contributor roles.

We can work with this fact, rather than dancing around it, by talking openly about the structure of the organization and how it impacts day-to-day operations. For example, how do we make decisions? We can ask and answer questions such as:

- Is this a democracy where the majority wins, or this a consensus-based culture?
- Do we have a leadership steering company or an executive team that ultimately makes decisions on behalf of the company?

- Are department or division leads empowered to make decisions about their own budgets, teams, or roadmaps without further approval? Or is additional sign-off required?
- Do hiring managers have final hiring sign-off, or is additional approval needed from HR or the executive team?
- Does the people operations team have autonomy to bring in outside programs, experts, and content—or is additional approval needed?
- Do managers have autonomy to terminate employment for underperforming team members—or do they need to work with HR or the personnel team?
- Do we need final sign-off from others, or can we move forward with decisions and report back?
- What decisions can the executive director make, and what decisions need to be reviewed and approved by the board?

It can be helpful to create clarity on these topics, and then to talk openly about them with our teams. This ties back to the idea that conflict is not a result of what happens or doesn't happen, but rather a result of misaligned expectations. Talking openly about these things can lead to more psychological safety *and* more trust. With this clarity in mind, team members will learn how the organization functions, how decisions are made, and how their input will be used along the way.

While there has been much conversation in recent years about psychological safety at work, we can also consider whether we are creating psychological safety within our personal lives. Consider:

- Am I creating psychological safety with my community members, neighbors, friends, and family members?
- Am I showing up in a way that allows my loved ones to feel accepted and respected even if they think or feel differently than I do about certain topics?
- Am I allowing my friends and loved ones to be their true selves—without fear of how I will behave or respond in return?

- Am I willing to love, and hold space for, people who might think and feel and vote differently than I do?

For a period of time, I had the pleasure of studying and teaching about Purpose, based on the research of The Blue Zones.[5] As part of this work, we examined what people said at the end of their lives.

Within this research, there were zero instances of people saying, "I'm really glad I cut out my friends and family who thought differently than I did" or "I'm really glad I spent so much time and energy trying to be right."

Rather, they said things such as, "I wish I would have prioritized my relationships," and "I wish I wouldn't have acted out of fear."

The invitation I offer you as we conclude this chapter is to consider: What is one thing that I can do to increase the psychological safety within my circles, and to create more space for people to be who they are without fear of judgment?

In moments when we feel triggered or angered by the actions of others, we might also take this as an opportunity to embrace our trusted practice of looking in the mirror—asking ourselves what needs to be resolved within our own hearts and minds and spirits, before we judge the hearts and minds and spirits of others.

EXPLORE

ABSENCE OF PSYCHOLOGICAL SAFETY	PRESENCE OF PSYCHOLOGICAL SAFETY
"Agreement" in the form of silence, for fear of speaking up	Spirited dialogue and discourse, rooted in respect and compassion
Heads down, eyes down	Heads up, eyes up
Everyone always agrees.	Disagreement is welcomed and discussed.
The energy of meetings and conversations shift dramatically depending on who is in the room.	The energy of meetings and conversations remains relatively consistent, regardless of who is in the room.
Team members don't speak up or contribute, for fear of repercussions.	Team members speak up and contribute openly and willingly.
We cut out people from our lives who don't think or believe the same things we do.	We love and accept the people in our lives who think or believe different things than we do.
We surround ourselves with people who have identical viewpoints and backgrounds.	We work to surround ourselves with people who have different perspectives, backgrounds, and life experiences.

REFLECT

1. How can I cultivate a feeling of psychological safety within my team, organization, and personal circles?

2. How can I support those whose voices are not being heard as loudly as mine?

3. What patterns, tendencies, or historical ways of functioning are diminishing the level of psychological safety for some individuals on our team? How can we begin to shift these ways of operating?

4. How can we measure the level of psychological safety on our team?

5. What am I unknowingly doing to reduce the level of psychological safety within my team or organization? How can I use this awareness to shift my behaviors accordingly?

BE SPECIFIC

Explicit disagreement is better than implicit misunderstanding.
—Douglas Stone and Sheila Hein

For the past three years, Rich has received feedback that he is negative. Rich doesn't see himself as negative, but rather as someone with a critical mind and an ability to spot, and then solve, problems. When he asks for clarification about this feedback, he hears something along the lines of, "It's just how you come across" or "It's something others have shared." This feedback is neither helpful nor actionable; it is an example that supports Gallup's findings that only 26 percent of employees strongly agree that the feedback they receive helps them do their work better.[6]

Over the years, I have observed a trend. Team members who feel overwhelmed and stressed-out often feel that way not because of the *amount* of work that they're doing, but because of a lack of clarity about *how* they're doing. Repeatedly, I've observed team members—especially those who are not part of the executive leadership team—running themselves into the ground, trying to achieve a level of excellent performance with no measurable finish line. In the absence of clearly defined expectations, the outcome is that these team members work *more*—leading them ultimately to burn out. In some cases, they are working harder at the wrong thing.

Conflict and frustration can be a product of ambiguity.

As leaders, we can work to reverse this trend and improve the meager 26 percent statistic by being specific. This means being clear and explicit with our expectations and then providing specific and actionable feedback.

The first step in this process is to identify, articulate, and communicate specific expectations. One way to do this is to think about the values of the organization and then to translate these into specific behaviors that reflect these values.

HINT

EXPECTATIONS = VALUES, TRANSLATED INTO
SPECIFIC ACTIONS AND BEHAVIORS

For example, if our organization has a value of respect, we can take this a step further to consider what respect looks like via actions and behaviors. We can write these things out for our colleagues and team members to reference. This allows everyone in the organization, at every level, to be crystal clear about what is expected and what this means in terms of specific and actionable behaviors.

Once we've defined our expectations, we can then provide feedback in a clear and specific way.

Many of us fall short when it comes to offering feedback. Giving helpful, constructive, and honest feedback can be incredibly challenging. Let's take a closer look at the feedback Rich received that he's negative.

What does that mean?

He doesn't consider himself a negative person. In fact, he is passionate about the success of his team and the company at large. The feedback that Rich is negative doesn't tell us anything specific, it doesn't give him anything upon which to improve, and it doesn't point him to a specific behavior or action that he can change in the future.

A better version of this feedback would be:

- In the client meeting on Thursday, I observed that you ended the meeting by telling our client what to do next. In the future, it could be helpful to frame this request as a question, by using "what" or "how" questions.
- In our retrospective last Wednesday, you shared that the client is being "a pain in the ass." While that might be true, those words landed harshly—especially with our more junior team members. In the future, you might frame this observation by clearly stating the challenges ("the client has not yet sent through their deliverable") and by talking through your plan ("and here's what I'm doing about it").
- In our training session on Monday, you audibly complained about your manager to a group of five peers. In the future, please share your feedback directly with your manager, as it is inappropriate to air these grievances in a setting such as a training session.

Being specific creates clarity for everyone involved. When offering feedback or input, this is particularly important. Once we start to listen for it, we will likely notice that squishy feedback abounds. Examples include:

- This person is negative.
- This person has a bad attitude.
- This person doesn't care.
- This person is unorganized.
- This person is unprofessional.
- This person has bad judgment.
- This person isn't ready for management.

- This person lacks confidence.
- This person isn't a strong communicator.

None of these statements provide actionable ways for people to improve. Additionally, this type of feedback is an interpretation, where we are taking the subjective liberty of interpreting not only how someone acted, but why they acted this way. As we explored previously in relation to making assumptions, this can be a slippery slope.

We can create clarity and reduce frustration by being specific. This means clearly articulating the values of the organization, translating what these values look like in the form of specific actions and behaviors, and then providing feedback that is based on behaviors and actions rather than on subjective interpretations.

No matter how thin, a pancake always has two sides. Our perspective is one side of the pancake. During these conversations, our opportunity is to hear about the other side of the pancake as well. Sometimes there is more to the situation than we might be aware of. We can leverage the skill of curiosity, which we explored in the previous section, to find out more.

An invitation: reflect on feedback that you've given recently—or feedback that you plan to give, and then translate this feedback to be *behavior or action based*. This can be much harder than we think, as much of our feedback for others typically contains some level of subjective interpretation.[7] You can try this with team members, colleagues, and even loved ones or children.

Here is a template that you can use to work toward feedback that is clear and actionable.

EXPECTATIONS:	ACTIONS AND BEHAVIORS:	OBSERVA-TIONS:
WHAT IS THE SPECIFIC EXPEC-TATION OF OUR TEAM, COMPANY, PROJECT, OR FAMILY?	WHAT DOES THIS EXPECTATION LOOK LIKE IN THE FORM OF SPECIFIC AND OBSERVABLE ACTIONS OR BE-HAVIORS?	WHAT SPECIFIC AND OBSERVABLE FEEDBACK DO I HAVE TO SHARE, THAT ROLLS UP TO THE CLEARLY COM-MUNICATED EXPEC-TATIONS?
For example: we have a company-wide value of Proactive Communi-cation.	*This means that we reply to client-facing emails within 48 hours.*	*I observed that you received three client inquiries last week that are unanswered. In service of our com-pany-wide value of Proactive Communi-cation and to maintain exceptional relation-ships, we aim to reply, even if in the form of a quick acknowledg-ment, within 48 hours. Can we talk about the emails from last week?*

INTERPRETIVE AND SUBJECTIVE FEEDBACK	CLEAR AND ACTIONABLE FEEDBACK
You always...	I observed...
You are...	I noticed...
You lack...	My expectation is...
This person is ...	Our shared value is ____. This looks like ____ in action. Here's how we can live this value through our everyday behaviors.
You do (or do not)...	The specific, observable behavior was...
You didn't do...	Here is what I observed. What is your perspective?

REFLECT

1. For feedback that I'm preparing to give, have I previously set clear expectations? If not, what could it look like to do so up front?

2. Where am I unintentionally drawing conclusions or making subjective interpretations about other people's behaviors? What could it look like to step out of this place of interpretation and into a place of giving clear, behavior-based feedback?

3. What are my expectations for colleagues and team members? Have I clearly communicated these?

4. What are our company values—and what do these look like when expressed as actions or behaviors?

5. Where might I be operating with implicit misunderstanding rather than explicit disagreement? What could it look like to get this conversation out into the open?

THE TRUTH HAS LEGS

The mistake most of us make in our crucial conversations is we believe that we have to choose between telling the truth and keeping a friend. We begin believing in the Fool's Choice from an early age.
—Kerry Patterson, Ron McMillan, Joseph Grenny,
Al Switzler, *Crucial Conversations*

I hadn't heard from Stacy in a week. This was unlike her; throughout the workshop series for university professionals, she had replied to follow-up prompts from the course with lightning speed. She commonly reached out with reflections about the topics. I wondered if something was wrong.

The following Monday morning, I sent her a text. "Hey Stacy," I said. "Just wanted to check in. I'm not sure if this is my intuition, or if I'm making up a story in my head, but I'm wondering if everything is okay. I'm sensing that it might not be."

I saw the [dot, dot, dot] of a text message in progress, and then it went away.

[Dot, dot, dot] was back again.

I felt a pit in my stomach.

After a few agonizing moments that felt like an hour, Stacy replied.

"I'd like to respond to the example you shared during the workshop last week. I have concerns about it."

At once, I was overcome with both relief and panic. Relief that I now knew why Stacy had been quiet for the last few days, but panic that I had unintentionally upset Stacy during the previous week's workshop. Stacy had been a longtime client and colleague whom I cared about and whom I was grateful to be working with through this university series. In addition to my fears about how the example may have unintentionally impacted our relationship, my people-pleasing saboteur—the one in me who *hates* unintentionally upsetting others—wanted to throw up.

"Want to hop on the phone to talk about it?" I asked.

The phone rang almost immediately.

We proceeded to have a twenty-minute conversation from a place of love and curiosity, during which we talked through each of our perspectives. While our perspectives were slightly different in relation to the example from class, there were also several threads of alignment. We hung up the phone, with each of us feeling simultaneously heard and relieved to have named the elephant in the metaphorical room. We talked about the issue that had been lingering in the space between us; we each told the truth with heart and held space for the other person to do the same.

Whether we are providing feedback, sharing our thoughts in a meeting, coaching team members, or giving an update to our board, our opportunity is to tell the truth with heart. This means that rather than dancing around the elephant in the room, we talk about it in a way that is both clear and kind. It invites us to practice both courage and openheartedness.

We can think of this idea as the following formula:

Truth + Heart = Courageous Leadership.

We can check in on each side of this equation.

TRUTH	HEART
Am I telling the truth?	Am I being kind?
Am I being honest?	Am I being compassionate?
Am I being clear?	Am I practicing empathy?
Am I speaking and acting with integrity?	Am I speaking from an "I" perspective, while also considering the other person's perspective and point of view?

When we speak in this way, through the prism of kindness, empathy, and compassion, it prevents us from needing to employ some of the less desirable methods that exist out there. These less desirable feedback delivery strategies include:

- Seagull-ing, which we covered previously
- Subjective interpretations
- The sandwich method, which means offering a compliment, followed by constructive feedback, followed by a complement[8]
- Pelting tomatoes, which is the opposite of the sandwich method— taking the tomatoes out of the metaphorical sandwich, and throwing them at another person

In talking with team members after receiving feedback via the methods above, I've heard many of them say, "What just happened here? Am I about to get fired or am I about to get promoted? I honestly have no idea if I'm doing an amazing job or if I'm totally messing things up." Or, they say, "I have no idea what I can actually do differently."

This is the danger of relying on these common feedback approaches. They can be squishy, they lack clarity, and they risk leaving those around us confused about the key takeaways from the conversation. Additionally, if we avoid the truth altogether, it creates a chasm that widens over time.

When preparing to tell the truth with heart, we might employ the twenty-four- and forty-eight-hour rule. Using this guideline, we can consider what we want to say for twenty-four hours by sleeping on the issue and giving it time to settle, but if there is something on our mind, we need to address it with in forty-eight hours. Once forty-eight hours pass, our window has expired. This prevents people from bringing up old issues, dwelling on baggage from the past, or holding resentments toward others over time. Can you imagine how different things could have been for both Bob and Heidi, as well as for Kyle's team, if they would have implemented this guideline?

We can tell the truth with heart by speaking from our own perspective, truthfully, with kindness, clarity, and compassion.

We can practice these phrases as we do:

- Here's what I'm noticing...
- Here's what I'm wondering...
- Here's what I'm observing...

By telling the truth with heart, we are practicing compassionate and courageous leadership and taking a stand for a more compassionate and courageous world.

The way to right wrongs is to turn the light of truth upon them.

—Ida B. Wells

HINT

TRUTH + HEART = COURAGEOUS LEADERSHIP

It can be uncomfortable to realize that the client we've been working with for the last four years is no longer a good fit for our organization. It can be painful to realize that our team member, despite tremendous amounts of coaching and mentoring, is not in the right role. It can be heartbreaking to come to terms with the fact that the start-up we joined four years ago is no longer the same company that it was and that we are no longer aligned with its mission and/or goals.

The truth has legs; it always stands. When everything else in the room has blown up or dissolved away, the only thing left standing will always be the truth. Since that's where you're gonna end up anyway, you might as well just start there.

—Rayya Elias

Telling the truth with heart means speaking clearly and with compassion. It means saying what needs to be said, from a place of kindness and empathy. It means naming the elephant in the room instead of dancing around it. It means being willing to look at and explore the truth even when it's difficult.

The truth can be scary—and painful. If we tiptoe around the truth, we don't have to look it in the eye. As a result, many of us—consciously or unconsciously—avoid the truth altogether.

As leaders, we can tell the truth with kindness and compassion. We can tell the truth in a way that is rooted in empathy and integrity. We can tell the truth in a way that is in service of the highest good of all.

To do so, we need to be grounded in ourselves and present to both the moment and the person before us. We need to be in relationship with reality rather than a version of reality that is in our head. And from here, from this calm and grounded and conscious place, we can tell the truth with heart.

This is not easy. As with everything in this book, it is a practice. We'll practice together.

Before we do, let's take a moment to reflect.

For you, what gets in the way of telling the truth with heart?

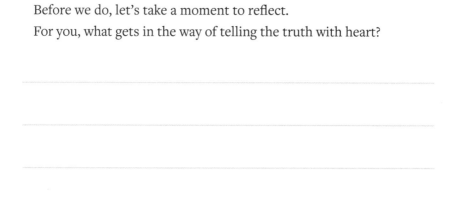

What do you know about yourself or these barriers? How are your areas of overfunctioning be getting in the way of your ability to tell the truth with heart?

One of my areas of overfunctioning shows up when I become so concerned about other people's needs, requests, and goals that I forget about my own. My colleague Beth astutely described this tendency as making accommodations, which happens any time that we take other people's needs or requests into account without also considering our own. One of my most frequent slip-ups happens when I try to squeeze things into my calendar, leading to calendar-related acrobatics on my end.

Shortly after starting my business, I started receiving emails from people who wanted to catch up or meet to pick my brain[9] over coffee. I am an extrovert, and I enjoy connecting via meaningful conversations with others, so I invariably accepted these invitations. Within a short time, my calendar was overtaken by these meetings. I remember one week trying to find time to have coffee with one of my closest friends and suggesting a date *eight weeks* into the future. I was prioritizing meetings with strangers or loose acquaintances over meetings with a friend who I had known since kindergarten. This was a problem.

In the year that followed, I started reducing the number of these meetings that I said yes to. With my calendar filled to the brim, I realized that I needed to make a choice: I needed to choose between time with my closest friends or time to meet with strangers and loose acquaintances.

While choosing the catch-up and pick your brain meetings may have been better for my business and appealed to the parts of my personality that love variety and meeting new people, choosing time with my closest friends was more aligned with my values.

While telling the truth with heart to strangers can be difficult, the most challenging opportunities may arise with those who we are closest to—colleagues, friends, and family members.

As we dive further into this section, I invite you to reflect again on what gets in your way when it comes to being completely truthful—with others and with yourself. You can write it down here and continue to check in with it as you read the pages that follow.

WHAT GETS IN THE WAY OF TELLING THE TRUTH WITH HEART?	WHAT AM I AFRAID OF?
Example: Fear of hurting or offending other people.	If I decline the "pick your brain" meeting to prioritize time with family and current clients, I am afraid that people will think I'm rude.
Example: Fear of emotional explosions.	If I tell my sometimes-volatile colleague how I feel, I'm afraid that he will explode and that the relationship will be damaged beyond repair.

EXPLORE

TRUTH *OR* HEART	TRUTH *AND* HEART
We chose between honesty and kindness.	We embrace both honesty and kindness.
We begin statements with "you always" or "you never."	We begin statements with "I'm noticing" or "I'm observing" or "my perspective is."
We water things down by being overly nice and rosy.	We are both clear and kind.
We rely solely on our own subjective interpretation of someone else's behavior.	We ask ourselves, "How can I create more clarity in this conversation?" We consider, "Am I clearly and kindly *saying what I mean?*"
We send passive-aggressive messages.	We pick up the phone or schedule time to talk.
We lob insults over the metaphorical fence.	We engage in compassionate and courageous dialogue.

REFLECT

1. What is one metaphorical elephant in the room that I'm currently dancing around? What could it look like to have a conversation *about* the elephant, rather than continuing to dance around it?

2. Where am I breaking the twenty-four- or forty-eight-hour rule—either speaking too quickly without thinking through my words or letting things fester for too long?

3. Where in my life or leadership am I not fully telling the truth? What could it look like to do so?

4. Where in my life or leadership could I benefit from more heart? What could it look like to lean into this?

5. Where do I tend to speak in a way that implies blame? What could it look like to shift toward an observation-based approach?

THE CONFLICT WE HAVE WITH OTHERS LIVES WITHIN US

If you are living your life and I am mentally living your life, who is here living mine? We're both over there. Being mentally in your business keeps me from being present in my own. I am separate from myself, wondering why my life doesn't work.

—Byron Katie

This section offers a bit of tough love. Much of the conflict that we think is about other people is often about us. Yes, that's right: much of the conflict that we think is about other people is *about us*.

Do you remember Reba from earlier in the book, who was infinitely frustrated with her team and organization? As you may recall, she almost fully resolved her inner conflict on this topic, even though very few things changed at work. She resolved the conflict with others by focusing on the conflict that lived within her.

Here, I'll invite you to think about an area of conflict or challenge in your work, leadership, or life. Perhaps you think about a particularly difficult conflict that pushes many of your buttons.

Now, just for a moment, tune into your own body. What are the thoughts, feelings, or assumptions that arise? What tension or sensations do you experience in your body? What part of this conflict lives within you?

Most likely, there is something that arises within you, even though you are not in the presence of the person or situation that is part of the conflict.

What this means is that much of the conflict that we assume is about others actually lives *within us*. For this reason, it is essential that we continue to practice the strategies in this book to deepen our self-awareness, work through our triggers, and do our own inner work so that we can first manage the conflict *within ourselves*, before we engage in conflict with others. This means continuing to check our assumptions, continuing to ask, "Is it true?" and noticing the thoughts, stories, and judgments that we are bringing into situations.

As Mary Oliver famously said, "To pay attention—this is our endless and proper work." Our endless and proper work as leaders is to continue to pay attention, not only to what's happening around us but to what's happening within us.

To build upon the words of Byron Katie, when we are busy worrying about everyone else, the lights are on, but nobody is home within our own house. We need to first tend to our own home before we look out the window at other people. Or, as my good friend and pro triathlete Jackie Hering says, "We need to water our own grass."

PROJECTING OUR CONFLICT ONTO OTHERS	EXPLORING THE CONFLICT THAT LIVES WITHIN US
Blame	Curiosity
Othering: we view or treat someone as intrinsically different than ourselves, and we alienate others.	Reflection: we recognize that oftentimes, that which triggers or infuriates us represents our own repressed shadow side. We get curious about these parts of ourselves.
Canceling or shutting out	Turning toward and looking within
Righteousness	Humility

REFLECT

1. What conflict that appears to be with others is actually conflict that lives within me?

2. What can it look like to do my own inner processing before I attempt to discuss or process with others?

3. When I am frustrated with another person, am I frustrated at a specific behavior or am I frustrated at the person for being who they are at their core?

4. When providing feedback to another person, am I asking them to shift a certain behavior or am I asking them to fundamentally change who they are?

5. Where might my perceived conflict about others be leading to a feeling of righteousness or othering? What can it look like to get curious about this?

BEING IN INTEGRITY
VERSUS BEING LIKED:
BE WILLING TO
WALK AWAY

At the end of the day, the only thing you take with
you when you're gone is your character.

—My dad

recently had a discovery call with a potential new corporate client. This
was a large conglomerate, made up of multiple companies around the
United States. Given the size, there was likely significant opportunity
for my business.

During this call, my colleague shared with me a few nuggets about how
they do business. Rather than paying for personality assessments that they
use with their team, she shared, they print them out, make photocopies,
and then recreate their own exact replica of the assessments in-house,
so that they don't have to buy additional through the official companies.

In other words, they regularly plagiarize the assessments and then distribute the plagiarized copies throughout the organization. They've been doing this for years.

This little nugget of information told me everything that I needed to know. Based on this example, I did not feel that this was a company that placed a high value on integrity, and therefore, it was not a company that I wanted to be associated with. I politely declined the invitation to submit recommendations or pricing. Even though it meant walking away from what could have been a large, high-dollar, ongoing contract, the answer was crystal clear.

A number of the executives and cofounders I coach face the question of whether to walk away when they realize that the start-up that they helped to create or helped to grow is no longer the company that they had joined or cofounded years before. The company that was once scrappy and agile and felt like a family is now bound by investor demands and muddled with reorgs and acquisitions. My colleague Lynn recently described her own situation of leaving the start-up that she'd cofounded "like getting a divorce, two weeks before having a baby."

Moving on from something that we've helped to grow or create is its own flavor of grief. Specifically, it is disenfranchised grief, a term that I learned from my colleague and friend Megan, who supports the dying and their families through death doula services. Disenfranchised grief is grief that isn't typically recognized by our society. It was first labeled by bereavement expert Kenneth Doka in 1989.[10]

While we might recognize the death of a parent or spouse as something to grieve over, we may overlook the grief that comes along with a transition away from a job or a company that we've been part of. As Lynn shared, when she talked with friends about her departure from her start-up, their response was "Great—you got a new job!" Inside, she was filled with sadness, hurt, and a profound sense of loss, as she had not only left her job but her family of other cofounders and the organization that she had helped to create.

I like to think of this as moving through a colored spectrum—from red, to orange, to yellow, to green—a concept that my beloved first coach, Carey, shared with me many years ago, when I was navigating my own departure out of the corporate world and into my business. While I had chosen to leave my job and was thrilled about starting my new business, there was an unsettled feeling of loss, grief, and confusion that I couldn't wrap my head around.

"Sarah," she said, as I shared how I was feeling. "You're just in the red right now. You'll get to the green, but it will take some time."

This framing provided a powerful visual that I refer to still today. When we leave something that we've invested a significant part of ourselves in, it feels as though we are in the red. Whether this is a project, a role, a company, a relationship, or our own start-up, the departure may be filled with a sense of grief, loss, and anxiety.

We can continue to raise our consciousness as leaders when we are not only willing to walk away from something that doesn't feel in integrity, but also when we are willing to acknowledge the pain and sadness that goes along with doing so. We can give ourselves grace, which then allows us to pass this grace along to others.

When Telling the Truth with Heart Doesn't Work

Sometimes, telling the truth with heart backfires.

I would be remiss to write this section and paint this process as all sunshine, blue skies, and roses. This can be incredibly difficult—and even if we do the work that we've explored in previous chapters, it might not be received well. It is still possible that things can blow up in our faces and that, in a worst-case scenario, we can fracture or even permanently sever relationships.

I will confess that over time, I've changed my tune on the topic of being truthful with heart. For many years, I believed that if we took the steps we've been exploring in earlier chapters, conversations would go well. My experience was that, overwhelmingly, this was the case. If we did our own inner work and came from a place of presence and compassion, even if we were talking about something difficult, we would eventually get to a good outcome. I still believe this to be true, when we are engaging with others who have done their own inner work, who have a stable core self, and who come to the conversation with a spirit of curiosity and compassion.

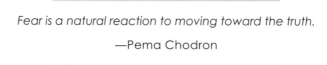

Fear is a natural reaction to moving toward the truth.

—Pema Chodron

I have realized over the years, however, that my previous approach was too optimistic and that it didn't solve for a number of factors, such as:

- People who haven't done any internal work, personal development, or inner reflection
- Individuals who have a fragile core self
- People with deeply rooted anger that comes out sideways (in this case, aimed at the teller of truth with heart)
- Individuals with certain personality disorders[11]
- Individuals who are in an altered state[12] during our conversation, unbeknownst to us
- Individuals who are emotionally, verbally, or even physically abusive
- People who have no interest in engaging in conscious and constructive dialogue

We don't know what other people are carrying with them in their metaphorical backpacks. We can't always predict whether we are stumbling into the territory of someone else's unhealed wounds.

As a result, we need to remember that these tools and skills are just that—tools and skills. And while we can use the tools to the best of our ability, doing so will not guarantee anything in terms of outcome or impact. We can only do the best we can with the tools we have—and we must remember that other people's tool kits can be unpredictable.

We may accidentally hit on one of the three feedback triggers outlined in *Thanks for the Feedback:*[13]

1. TRUTH: the other person doesn't think the feedback is true.
2. RELATIONSHIP: *we* are the problem, and no matter what we say, it isn't going to land well, if it comes from us.
3. IDENTITY: we unknowingly bring up a sensitive or unhealed part of someone's identity through the feedback that we share (this can produce the most volatile result, I've found).

So while we can do everything we can to refine our skills and use these tools and show up from a place of integrity, grace, and compassion, we cannot—and should not try to—predict the way that others will respond or attach too much to the outcome. This is easier said than done, of course.

An astute colleague says, "Everyone is doing the best they can with what they have on board. . . and, we don't always know what others have on board."

If you do have an uncomfortable blow-up with a colleague or team member, here are some practical steps you can take toward healing, recovery, and, ultimately, peace.

- MEDITATING: focusing on meditations that are rooted in loving kindness, Tonglen (taking in other people's pain while sending them relief), or cord cutting (a visualization in which we cut energetic cords with another person or situation)
- DEEP BREATHING: lengthening the exhale to be slightly longer than the inhale
- RELEASING: asking, "What can I let go of? How can I carry forward the lessons of this interaction, while releasing what doesn't serve me?"

- LOOKING IN THE MIRROR: considering, "What can I learn about myself from this situation?"
- ACKNOWLEDGING OURSELVES: for having the courage to tell the truth with heart, no matter the outcome
- PRACTICING COMPASSION AND EMPATHY: toward ourselves and the other person or people involved
- ENGAGING THE HELP OF A PROFESSIONAL: a coach, therapist, mentor, or trusted colleague for outside perspective
- PUTTING DOWN THE METAPHORICAL MIRROR: recognizing that in some situations and relationships, resolution is not possible. The problem is no longer about us. Little heartfelt communication lands with those who are not willing to do their own self-reflection and take responsibility for their side of the street. In these cases, we accept that we've done all that we can do and work to release the grips of the situation or the other person.

EXPLORE

BEING LIKED	BEING IN INTEGRITY
We do what is easy or popular.	We do what is right.
We grovel.	We are kind, while also being grounded in our strong and steady center.
We spend our time and energy trying to fix other people's metaphorical houses.	We spend our time first fixing our own house and watering our own grass.
We compromise our values and integrity.	We stand in our values and integrity.

REFLECT

1. Where do I need to walk away?

2. Where am I trying to be liked, rather than being in integrity?

3. Where am I trying to tell the truth with heart to a person who might not be able to receive it?

4. Where might I currently be triggered by one of the three feedback triggers?

5. Where might one of my colleagues or team members be triggered? How can I adjust my approach accordingly?

BE CREATIVE:

LEAD WITH AGILITY

BE ANCHORED TO WHAT
MATTERS WHILE BEING
LIGHT ON YOUR FEET

If change is the only constant, let's get better at it.

—Jenny Blake

This book had been teetering around 85 percent completion for weeks. Writing the book started to feel hard and heavy. I continued plugging along, staring at the page with dread and confusion. What was going on, and why did the process feel so hard?

I often feel most creative and inspired when I am working in a new location. In an attempt to make progress and connect to a jolt of insight, I took myself on a short getaway to work on the book in a new city. After a couple of days of slogging along in this new physical location, it hit me: I had been writing the book for the slightly wrong audience. Rather than writing this book for the conscious, heart-centered, and highly impactful leaders who I primarily work with, I was trying to write this book in a way that would appeal to *all types of leaders.* Of course, trying to appeal to everyone ends up looking an awful lot like appealing to no one. In my attempt to write the book for too broad of an audience, I had become disconnected from my own authentic voice.

While it would have been much easier to ignore my little getaway epiphany and finish the remaining 15 percent, it wasn't the path forward that felt true to me. Additionally, it wouldn't have felt delightful or inspiring; it would have continued to feel burdensome.

As a result of this insight, I started over. I rewrote the entire book, from the beginning, in my own authentic voice, and with my inspiring target reader in mind. This was, of course, much more work, and it pushed back the publication date, but it led to a book that I am proud of.

Recent years have given us plenty of opportunity to practice being agile.

Our world continues to change before our eyes. Each time it feels like we have settled in, even for a moment or two, things change. Whether through pandemics and lockdowns, fires and floods, school closings, unexpected layoffs, mergers and acquisitions, or a new CEO with a new vision for the company, most of us have been forced to embrace agility in some form or another in recent years. Agility allows us to create from whatever is happening around us, even if what is happening is unexpected or unintended. Agility means having a plan, while also being light enough on our feet to adapt and respond to our current reality.

Agility means being grounded in ourselves, our integrity, and our values, while also being open to the needs of others and the world around us. We can think of this as being anchored to what matters, while being light on our feet.

Leadership agility, in its simplest terms, is the ability to anticipate and respond to change.

In times of change, turmoil, unrest, and confusion, we need to remain connected to our core with our feet on the ground, while simultaneously being light enough on our feet to respond to what is happening around us. As we connect to our why and purpose, we can consider:

- What matters?
- What is important?
- What is this all about?

How many times have you been in a meeting, where people started throwing out ideas on what to do next, without considering *why* they were doing them or *what* this was all in service of?

A few years ago, I was in a meeting for a volunteer project that went something like this:

- We could have monthly meetings!
- We could have quarterly meetings!
- We could do projects!
- We could have guest speakers!
- We could have recurring speakers!
- We could do happy hours!
- We could have breakfast meetings!

You get the idea. The meeting went on like this for a rather painful hour and a half. Finally, we raised the essential questions: "What is our why? What is our purpose? What are we trying to accomplish?"

While we didn't figure out those answers right then and there, it did lead us to pause the enthusiastic brainstorming to attempt to consider why we were coming up with these ideas in the first place.

Typically, our *why* remains relatively constant while the *how* and *what* may be dynamic and evolving. Our *why* can guide us, provide clarity about the decisions that we make, and serve as a North Star. It serves as our stake in the ground that we can continually revisit.

I like to visualize this stake in the ground as a physical stake that we can hold onto and that we can come back to if we are drifting away. Our stake anchors us to what matters and what is important.

The topic of innovation has become increasingly popular. Many organizations have embraced the idea, with some companies creating innovation departments and innovation leads. While this can be successful when done well, one of the biggest hurdles I see is a lack of a clear purpose and why. A number of organizations and teams are excited to innovate and create positive change, but they are unclear on their core why and purpose. This can lead to a multitude of ideas that lack implementation and execution, and in a worst-case scenario, it results in a frustrated and disengaged team. Before we start brainstorming, tossing out ideas, or stirring up new initiatives, we first must step back and connect to our core why and purpose.

I have several colleagues who have practiced agility in the form of re-designing their teams. My friend Tim is a contractor. He loves building things and the simplicity of being what he calls a one-man show. Over the years, under the advice of well-meaning friends and colleagues in the field, he found himself building a team. Suddenly, he looked around and had a team of nine. His days were no longer spent building things but rather managing payroll and personnel issues. He felt disconnected from the work, from his core purpose, and his sense of joy. In the years that followed, he deconstructed his team and went back to being a one-man show. He still brings in others, but nowadays, as freelancers. This provides him the best of both worlds. He can collaborate with others, while maintaining the joy, freedom, and agility that he finds in his tiny, one-man team.

During a recent visit to a local restaurant chain that specializes in fresh, local, and healthy on-the-go options, I noticed that smoothies were no longer on the menu. When I inquired about this with the manager, he shared, "Smoothies accounted for less than 20 percent of our revenue, but they accounted for over 80 percent of our headaches! The blenders are loud, the fruit takes a long time to cut up, and it takes three times as long to make a smoothie as it does a salad. Plus, whenever the blenders would leak, which was often, it created a huge mess, which took time and energy away from serving our customers. While people loved our smoothies, we decided to take them off the menu. Our business has been running so much more efficiently ever since!" This restaurant manager had stumbled upon the Pareto Principle, which is the idea that 80 percent of consequences come from 20 percent of causes, and he decided to pivot accordingly. This allowed the restaurant team to stay anchored to their core mission of offering healthy local food, while being light on their feet to eliminate the product offering that wasn't serving the business.

Every morning we wake up and come to see that we do not face the world, because the world is always waking up through us.

—Michael Stone

Being light on our feet means being anchored to our core why and purpose, while remaining open and responsive to the world around us. From here, we can consciously create what is needed in the moment. We can work with the world around us rather than fighting against it.

We will be faced with this choice as leaders. We can continue along the path that we are on, even if it doesn't feel right or make sense based on the clues that we're getting, or we can pivot based on the information that we have in the moment before us.

EXPLORE

RIGIDITY	AGILITY
We feel helpless.	We continually create from our current reality.
We want to stick to the plan even if the plan is no longer serving us.	We are willing to adapt and shift based on what is needed in this current moment.
The Pareto Principle (also known as the 80/20 rule) is in play in the wrong direction, but we are either not aware of it or unwilling to examine it further.	We examine the various expressions of the Pareto Principle within our life and business. Where are 20 percent of the causes creating 80 percent of the results? And what needs to shift accordingly?
It feels like life is happening *to* us.	We spot opportunities, even within the obstacles.

REFLECT

1. What is working well in my work and our life? What isn't working as well?

2. Where is a greater level of agility needed as a result?

3. Where am I holding tightly as part of a plan that may no longer be relevant?

4. Where is the Pareto Principle at play within my own life or business—a situation where 80 percent of issues, headaches, or client complaints are rooted in 20 percent of offerings, products, or decisions? What could it look like to examine the root cause and consider making a shift accordingly?

5. On the flip side, what are the 20 percent of my offerings, products, or decisions that are creating 80 percent of positive results? What could it look like to invest further in these?

SWIM WITH THE CURRENT

Divine Order says that the perfect solution to any problem is already selected if you allow yourself to be guided; Divine Source says there is a natural Universal Abundance that knows how to meet every need.

—Tosha Silver

---

visited my local botanical garden and paused to watch the fish. The giant, orange fish floated effortlessly in the pond, surrounded by lush greenery and brightly colored plants. The fish weren't *trying* to float; they were floating.

The brown trout in the local stream do the same. They swim with the current, effortlessly gliding along through the crystal-clear water.

Do you ever feel as though you are swimming against the current? Swimming upstream, putting forth tremendous amounts of effort and strength, only to move a couple of centimeters? When we feel as though we are swimming upstream, this can be a signal that something needs to shift. There is a difference between working hard and swimming upstream. Working hard may feel like we are in a state of flow. We are creating impact in the world, and the world is responding. Swimming upstream, on the other hand, feels like we are *trying* to create impact in the world, using every ounce of our energy, but getting nowhere.

We talked in the last section about the fact that conflict is data which informs us that something wants to emerge, shift, or change within a system[1] or a relationship. The same is true when we face conflict in the form of swimming upstream. Our opportunity as leaders is to look for the clues and then to make changes accordingly.

When we feel like we are working hard but making little progress, this is a clue that we need to pause, look around, and consider what could shift. Sometimes the shift comes from us—a shift in our approach, our perspective, or our way of thinking about the problem. Sometimes the shift comes from others—for example, by asking for help, by partnering with another organization to collaborate, or by hiring a new team member. Sometimes the shift comes from looking around at our environment or context for clues, listening expansively, and paying attention to what comes back. As we explored earlier, the metaphorical cistern is always playing music back to us.

What if leadership was one big rafting expedition—with your team members, your colleagues, with friends and family, and with the larger world around you? And what if, rather than constantly paddling against the current or swimming upstream, you could regularly lead from a place of flow?

This is possible. It doesn't mean that it will always be easy, but it does mean that we get to choose how to be in relationship with the world around us. It is also more fun and more effective, if we choose to be *in* relationship with the world around us, rather than fighting against it.

As leaders, our opportunity is to be in a constant dance with the people and the world around us so that we can consciously create the next steps. This means choosing to engage in the world from the perspective of "I am in relationship with the world around me," rather than "the world is conspiring against me." It means leaning into reality, rather than fighting against it. It means practicing personal agency and consciously creating from our world and the moments before us. And it means paying attention to the many clues that surround us each day.

Here is what swimming with the current might look like.

On a recent trip, I had a 10:00 a.m. checkout time and an 8:45 p.m. flight. I wasn't sure what I was going to do with those extra hours, and the forecast was calling for heavy rain. I researched many options, from renting an office for the day to extending my current accommodations (which were booked), to securing another type of space, but none of these options felt right. The process felt *hard*. Forced. Like it wasn't meant to be. So instead of taking any further action, I put out an intention that the perfect opportunity would present itself. In other words, I didn't book anything and instead chose to wing it, trusting that something would work out.

A few days into my trip, I was texting with my friend Helen and told her what state I was in. She said, "If you're in this city, be sure to call Sabine—she lives here now!" I couldn't believe it. I was in one of the largest states in the United States, and it just so happened that our beloved mutual friend had recently moved there. I texted her, and we immediately started making plans for my free day. While I had suggested a walk from her house, she said, "Well, what are you going to do for the day? Come on over to my house. You can work outside, we can hang out here for the day, and we can have dinner together before you head out. It will be perfect."

And it was. Instead of spending the day running around between rented coworking spaces or random accommodations, I spent the day with my friend, in her gorgeous backyard, catching up on life, eating delicious local food, and meeting her wonderful husband for the first time. The day was more perfect than anything I could have imagined and turned out to be a highlight of my year.

I had to let go of trying to figure out how it was *supposed to be* and instead open myself up to the possibility of how it *could be*, for this opportunity to present itself. I had to allow myself to be unattached to the outcome for the perfect solution to arise. And, as a bonus, it ended up being a gorgeous, sunny day.

I had a similar experience when I felt ready to leave my job many years ago. I started looking at other possibilities and interviewing for other positions. At one point, I considered taking another job, which would have involved a 45-minute commute, driving to the opposite end of the city each day to work on a project that I wasn't terribly interested in. I considered accepting the offer, but I knew intuitively that I would have been forcing it. None of the opportunities I had found to date were right. I wanted to be running *toward* something that was aligned with my future vision, and not just *away* from something that no longer felt like a fit.

As I was looking at other positions, I could have never imagined that the opportunity I was supposed to take would not involve another job at all, but rather, it would involve starting my own business. I had to loosen my grip in order for this clarity to emerge. It took over three years for clarity to arise, but when it did, it struck me like a bolt of lightning, and I knew with complete and total certainty that this was my path. This happened only after I allowed myself to become slightly detached from the "right" path and opened myself up to a more expansive set of possibilities.

The world works in mysterious ways, as they say. And as leaders, we can lean into the mystery, get curious about it, and explore the ways in which it is guiding us toward the answers that we seek. By doing this, we are often more successful and more effective, and our lives and our leadership begin to feel more joyful. One of my teachers, Sam, used to frequently say, "Oh, goodie!" to describe a possible reaction to something unexpected that is happening around us.

Being in relationship with the world around us is a continuous practice of saying, "Oh, goodie!"

EXPLORE

SWIMMING AGAINST THE CURRENT	SWIMMING WITH THE CURRENT
We feel as though we are pushing against the world around us.	We feel as though we are in relationship with the world around us.
We reject new information or data points and continue to push forward.	We incorporate new information and data points and allow our journey to be shaped by what we learn.
We push against the current.	We pause to yield to the current when needed.
We externalize our world: things happen *to* us. We are helpless. There's nothing we can do.	We practice agency within our world: we consider opportunities to create from whatever is happening. There's almost always something we can do.

REFLECT

1. What are the ways in which I could lean into the world around me, rather than fighting against it?

2. What is one small but meaningful shift that I could make to start swimming with, rather than against, the current?

3. What is one example from the past where the world was on my side?

4. Where am I working harder on the wrong thing?

5. Where would it make sense to pause and yield to the current?

ZOOM UP: TAKE THE HELICOPTER VIEW

The environment is where we all meet, where we all have a mutual interest; it is the one thing all of us share. It is not only a mirror of ourselves, but a focusing lens on what we can become.

—Lady Bird Johnson

During a recent leadership program, Jeremy, the IT lead for a software company, expressed frustration over an issue that he was navigating. "With Angie's recent departure," he said, "we are learning about all sorts of sites that only she had access to. I'm in the process of trying to find all of them, deactivate accounts accordingly, and figure out how we will access these accounts in the future."

As we continued to talk about the issue, we experimented with zooming up, which we will call taking the Helicopter View. When taking the Helicopter View, we imagine that we are up in a helicopter, looking down not only at the issue but at the surroundings, the landscape, and the people who are involved. From up here, we can see the issue not as an isolated incident but as part of a larger system and part of a greater whole.

The group collectively zoomed up to look at Jeremy's issue from the helicopter view. As we did, other members of the group nearly gasped. "Oh my gosh," Cody, another participant said. "This is happening all over the company. On my team, Andre is the only one who has access to our after-hours codes, and he is the only one who knows how to operate this massive database. It works okay, because Andre is awesome and is very responsive…but what will we do if something happens to Andre or if he isn't available?"

"This recently came up for me, as well," said Asher, a design lead on the team. "Last week, our team member Taylor lost power and internet for two weeks due to the winter storms. It was the first time that we had to figure out how to navigate a completely unplanned outage for one of our team members."

As the group continued to talk, they realized that what Jeremy had unearthed as an isolated access issue due to an employee's departure was much bigger than it originally seemed—in fact, not an isolated issue at all. The group recognized, through the thoughtful discussion that followed, that the *real* issue was about company resiliency and redundancy. Across the company, how can they ensure that there are backups, systems, and structures in place in the event of departures, outages, and other unforeseen events?

The group was able to uncover the real issue by zooming up and looking down at the system from the helicopter view. From here, they were able to see not only Jeremy's issue but the related issues across the organization. They also discovered, through this exploration, that there was another piece to this puzzle. Because team members were busy and stretched thin, there was a habit of solving the issue at hand as quickly as possible to check it off the list, rather than pausing, stepping back, and considering the larger threads or impacts.

As part of a scrappy company that was once a small start-up, team members were accustomed to working hard, solving the immediate issue at hand, then moving on. As the company had grown and the complexity of issues continued to increase, they determined that they needed to have a larger conversation about the ways in which this was happening across the organization.

In our own teams, organizations, and lives, we can look for opportunities to zoom up and take the helicopter view.

EXPLORE

LOOKING DOWN	ZOOMING UP
Looking at issues in isolation	Looking at issues in the context of the whole
Singular	Collective
Alone	Connected
Check it off the list	Consider: who else will be impacted by this?

REFLECT

1. What issues am I facing that could benefit from The Helicopter View?
2. What does the view look like from up here?
3. From this view, what is needed?
4. What other issues or data points are related?
5. How can I lead most effectively within this system?

REDIRECT THE FIREHOSE

In the absence of time to physically and politically engage with our community the way many of us want to, the internet provides a cheap substitute: it gives us brief moments of pleasure and connection, tied up in the opportunity to constantly listen and speak. Under these circumstances, opinion stops being a first step toward something and starts seeming like an end in itself.

—Jia Tolentino, *Trick Mirror*

Maci is a passionate advocate. She cares about animals, the environment, women's rights, peace in the Middle East, breaking glass ceilings and smashing the patriarchy, mental health, creating employment opportunities for people who were previously incarcerated, veganism, and local food systems, just to name a few.

For the last three years, Maci has spent several hours online each day reposting content about each of these causes. Her social media feeds are a constant stream of alarming news headlines, heartbreaking photos, and videos from other activists working on these causes.

One Tuesday morning, Maci unexpectedly passed out at 11:00 a.m. She went to the doctor, did blood tests, and saw a therapist. The culprit? Exhaustion.

Maci had been spending a tremendous amount of energy spraying the firehose. Maci was holding onto the firehose with all her strength, while it was cranked up to full blast and spraying in all directions. She was spraying the firehose at everything she was concerned about, rather than focusing it on the things that she could impact, influence, shift, or change in some way.

After a few days of rest, Maci decided on a new path forward. Rather than spending three hours per day posting about all of these causes, she would spend two hours each week volunteering in person with a local organization that employees previously incarcerated individuals on local farms—combining two of her passions and allowing her to make a direct and meaningful impact.

After just two weeks, Maci noticed a significant improvement to her energy, mood, and overall sense of well-being. She even decided to do a two-week social media hiatus, deleting all of her apps from her phone. She formed deep relationships with both the other volunteers and also the employees on the farm. Several friends told her that she was suddenly glowing.

Maci's example invites us to consider where in our work or life we are spraying the firehose in all directions, but with little actual impact. Where are we spending excessive amounts of time or energy being concerned about, upset by, or angered by things that are happening externally? What if, instead, we redirected that time and energy to consider the things that we can impact, influence, shift, or change in some way?

We can think about this as taking conscious action, which is a concept that we explored earlier in the book. Here, you might consider what this breakdown looks like for you.[2] What are you passionate about, where are you currently spraying the firehose or being swept away by the current, and what could it look like to move toward conscious and intentional action?

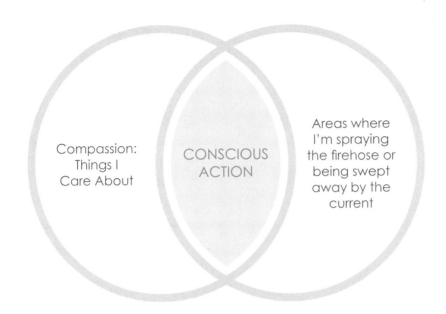

Compassion: Things I Care About

CONSCIOUS ACTION

Areas where I'm spraying the firehose or being swept away by the current

Leading with agility invites us to look around, examine what is needed, and then consider how we can show up and lead given what we have discovered. There is a difference between being concerned or upset by something and taking meaningful action. Our opportunity is to look for the areas of potential action, even if they are small. With clients, the first action is usually not to solve the whole problem, but rather a more discrete task such as setting up a meeting, calling a colleague, writing down a list of specific concerns, or blocking thirty minutes on the calendar to think through a plan.

And as for Maci? She's still volunteering with the local organization and has increased her time on the farm from two to four hours each week. While she spends a couple of hours per week on social media, she only visits the websites on her laptop and has left all the apps off her phone. When reflecting on the situation, she says, "Passing out that morning was a gift; it was a wake-up call that I had been running myself into the ground without actually changing anything. Now, whenever I find myself veering toward exhaustion, I stop to consider what is within my realm of influence and how I can start there."

EXPLORE

SPRAYING THE FIREHOSE	REDIRECTING THE FIREHOSE
Feeling angered, triggered, or frustrated by a large number of issues	Deciding which of the issues matter most and considering how to take concrete action on at least one of them
Trying to solve all of the issues at the same time	Pausing to consider: where can I make the greatest impact? How can I most effectively direct my time, talents, and energy?
Conflating posting (for example, on social media) with acting	Doing a gut check: If I am posting about something that bothers me, am I also taking action out in the real world?
Feel Good—by posting, being outraged, or yelling into an echo chamber	Do Good—by taking concrete action in service of the things we care about most

REFLECT

1. Where in my work or life am I spraying the firehose? What is the impact?

2. What is one item on my current list of concerns? What, related to that concern, can I impact, influence, shift, or change in some way?

3. Where on my team or within my organization are we collectively spraying the firehose? What could it look like to shift toward focused action?

4. What is one thing I can do to get involved with a cause or issue that I care about?

5. How can I expand the center by making my circle of influence bigger?

TAKE THE THIRD PATH

K
ennedy came to our coaching session feeling conflicted. "I'm just not sure," she said, "if I should look for a new role, or if I should stay home with my kids for a little while longer."

Kennedy had been at her previous role for eight years. While she loved many parts of it, the hours and the travel weren't conducive to the balance she was seeking with her family.

"What if we could find a way for both?" I asked.

In the conversation that followed, Kennedy proceeded to map out her ideal structure. It would involve a thirty-two-hour workweek, working Monday through Thursday, and staying home with her kids on Fridays. It would also be a role that included leadership responsibilities, as Kennedy loved managing and coaching others.

"Those things don't typically go together," she said. "It doesn't seem possible to both be in a leadership role *and* work less than forty hours per week; not a lot of companies are open to that."

"Let's just see," I said.

In the weeks that followed, we proceeded to write up an ideal job description. Kennedy mapped out her desired set of responsibilities, the ways in which she felt she could have the greatest impact, and her ideal thirty-two-hour Monday-through-Thursday schedule. Once the job description felt complete, she started her search.

Kennedy received a call back from a rapidly growing company in town that was looking for a technical support lead. During her interview, she brought a printed copy of her ideal job description, thinking that it would be a long shot.

A few days after the interview, the hiring manager called her back, not only offering her the exact position that she had pitched, but at a salary that was 30 percent higher than what she was expecting.

It can be easy to think that we have two options: should I stay at my job, or should I leave? Should I say yes to the opportunity to relocate abroad, or should I turn it down? Should I accept the offer, or should I decline? Should I stay in my current neighborhood, or should I move?

Oftentimes, what we think is either/or is anything but. There is a Third Path—a path of both/and.

We can stay at our job but update our resume and start to have some conversations about what else is out there. We can remain at our job and start a side hustle. We can take the new opportunity, on contract for three months, to try it out. We can do a pilot or a trial before we commit fully. We can counteroffer or negotiate. We can rent a house in the other neighborhood that we're considering across town, to experience what it's like to live there for a week.

There are rarely just two options. Our continuous opportunity is to look for the Third Path, the additional possibility, the expanded set of options. The Third Path often exists if we are willing to look for it.

EXPLORE

EITHER/OR	BOTH/AND
It is choice A or choice B.	What is a less obvious option C?
It is yes or no; black or white.	It is yes *and*. It is multi-color.
Pro/con	Pro/pro^3 or con/con—we expand the ways in which we are looking at *all* options, in order to open up new possibilities.

REFLECT

1. What current questions in my work or life could benefit from a Third Path?

2. In what areas of my work or life am I using either/or thinking? What could it look like to think bigger?

3. What are some Third Paths that exist for questions or decisions I'm currently working through?

4. How might I shift my meeting agendas or communication strategies to create space to explore the Third Path?

5. What current problems, frustrations, or irritations in my life could be remedied by considering a Third Path?

THE ELUSIVE MIDDLE: LOVE WHAT IS AND MAKE THINGS HAPPEN

It is not enough to fight for the land; it is even more important to enjoy it. While you can. While it's still here. So get out there and hunt and fish and mess around with your friends, ramble out yonder and explore the forests, climb the mountains, bag the peaks, run the rivers, breathe deep of that yet sweet and lucid air, sit quietly for a while and contemplate the precious stillness, the lovely, mysterious, and awesome space.

—Edward Abbey

Mac is a successful leader in the tech industry who has his dream job—a role that was created specifically for him, in which he's able to use his gifts of strategic thinking, collaboration, and problem solving. Mac and his wife are joyfully adjusting to life with a toddler and recently welcomed a sweet rescue dog into their home. In a recent coaching conversation, Mac asked,

"How can I actually let myself *enjoy* a good job?"

His question was powerful, not only in what it represented for him as an individual but in the way that it represents somewhat of a fundamental human challenge: How can we appreciate and enjoy what we have, what we've created, and the very thing that we most wanted, without continually looking over the fence at what else is out there or what's next?

Do any of these actions feel familiar?

- You recently moved into a new space that you love but find yourself secretly perusing new property listings on your phone late at night.
- You recently received a promotion at work but find yourself already thinking about what's next after this.
- You recently landed your dream role with a company that closely aligns with your values but have been regularly checking other job listings just in case there is something better out there.
- You exceeded your revenue goals, and rather than taking a moment to pause and celebrate, you quickly move on to defining *next year's* revenue goals—which will be even bigger and better.
- You accomplished everything on your list, and instead of taking a tiny break, you make a new list.

In my coaching work with clients, I observe that many of us are continuously trying to find the Elusive Middle—the place that exists between striving, grinding, taking action, getting things done, grasping, and wanting *more*; and being in the moment, practicing gratitude, mindfulness, presence, and acceptance for what *is*.

Part of leadership agility involves finding our way toward this tricky-to-locate place—the place in between massive action and complete acceptance. It invites us to practice acceptance for *what is,* while taking action toward *what can be.* When we are running too fast, without pausing along the way, we, too, can find ourselves facing burnout and exhaustion. And when our acceptance skews too far toward complacency, we can find ourselves at the mercy of the world around us.

Complacency   Settling   Inability to
Create Change   Feeling Helpless

Being in
the Moment

Pausing   Reflecting   Presence

Acceptance   Mindfulness

THE
ELUSIVE
MIDDLE

Taking Action   Looking Ahead

Seeking
Challenges   Focusing on
What Is Next

Getting
Things Done

Grinding   Striving   Difficulty Being
in the Moment   Never Satisfied

Exploring the Elusive Middle is not only a practice in agility, but also in self-compassion. It's a way to honor our natural tendencies, while keeping what serves us and letting go of the rest. It is an opportunity to practice operating in the middle, to hold the idea of both/and. It is an invitation to allow ourselves to exhale, to be where we are, and to appreciate the reality that is before us. It's a practice of both the *being* and the *doing* that we explored earlier in the book. As leaders, we need both.

What can it look like to step into the middle and hold both?

LOVING WHAT IS AND BEING HERE NOW	THE ELUSIVE MIDDLE	MAKING THINGS HAPPEN AND LOOKING AT WHAT'S NEXT
Presence	Mindful action	Growth
Appreciation	Compassionate self-inquiry	Challenge
Loving what is		Pushing
Being here now	Conscious choice	Crafting a vision for the future
Acceptance	Movement and rest	
Stillness	Work and play	Innovation and creation
Mindfulness		Action
Pause		Stretching
		Looking ahead

REFLECT

1. Where do I tend to fall along this continuum—do I lean more toward action or stillness?

2. What are the gifts of my natural tendency?

3. Where in my life am I leaning too far toward the right and experiencing a sense of grinding, striving, or grasping?

4. Where am I leaning too far to the left and experiencing a sense of complacency or inaction?

5. What could it look like to embrace the gifts of both sides and practice stepping into the Elusive Middle?

CREATE FROM
THIS MOMENT

*How wonderful it is that nobody need wait a single
moment before starting to improve the world.*

—Anne Frank

t is a beautiful June morning. The sun is shining, the birds are chirping, and Cecilia is sitting at her favorite outdoor cafe surrounded by her three most trusted girlfriends: Monique, Whitney, and Amber. They are sharing a carafe of dark roast and a plate of scones; they had cut them into fourths so that they could sample all of the flavors. They meet monthly before work to catch up on work and life and to talk through their trickiest leadership challenges together. While they all work in different industries, they appreciate the sisterhood, support, and outside perspective that these monthly gatherings provide.

After a bite of the blueberry scone, Monique asks, "So, Cecilia, how *are* you? And how is work? The last time we met, you had your hands full with the quality issue, your departing team member, and a lot of late nights in a row."

"You're not going to believe it," Cecilia said, "but things are incredible. This is what I've been up to." She smiled as she held up a beautiful leather notebook, with a page titled *Regular Leadership Actions* bookmarked via a purple ribbon. She displayed her list and offered a brief description of each item.

- WORKOUTS: I reinstituted my morning workouts—twenty minutes of either yoga or walking before the workday—which helps me to show up in a more present and grounded way with my team.

- ASSUMPTIONS: Prior to important meetings and conversations, I clear out my assumptions and ask myself "is it true?" to work through stories in my head that are getting in my way. This practice has not only helped me to be more present in conversations, but it made me realize that I was holding all sorts of false beliefs about what leadership was supposed to look like—from how I thought I had to act, to what leaders were supposed to wear to work. After a few weeks of doing this exercise, I even got rid of my heels and switched over to more comfortable shoes, which now allows me to easily schedule midday walking meetings with my team members. Getting out of the office and into the fresh air has made such a difference!

- BEGINNING AND END OF DAY CHECK-IN: I do a quick check-in on the type of impact I'd like to make during the day, and then before wrapping up at the end of the day, I ask myself what I did well and what I could have done better as a leader. I'm learning so much by simply pausing to check in with myself on a regular basis.

- MEETINGS: We've restructured our team meetings to be forty-five minutes instead of two hours, and we start every single one by anchoring to our core why and purpose. It has made us more productive and has created a ripple effect of energy on the team. Plus, we've all gained back over an hour of time to get heads-down work done.

- COACHING: Rather than doing hour-long task-based meetings with my team members, I've switched up the format to be weekly thirty-minute coaching sessions. Team members bring their topics, and instead of taking on all of my team members' metaphorical monkeys, I listen, ask questions, and then empower them to move forward after our conversations.
- HARD STUFF: I forced myself to have the hard conversation with our CEO that I'd been avoiding for the last three months. It was a stretch, but I told the truth with heart, and we are restructuring the entire division as a result. It went much better than I could have predicted, and the team is already starting to work more effectively together.
- COMMUNICATION: We have implemented a new quarterly cross-functional division leads meeting so that department leads can learn from each other and so that people aren't solving similar issues in isolation. Just for fun, we named the meeting "Quarterly Helicopter Ride" as a reminder to continue to zoom up, get out of the weeds, and remember that we are rarely alone with the issues that we are trying to solve.

Cecilia took a breath between her excited explanation and then proceeded, "I feel like I'm much more impactful as a leader, and the team shared that they feel more impactful too. Most importantly, I feel more *free*. I've even started cooking again—something I love but that I wasn't making time for during this busy stretch. Overall, it's been a great month."

Monique, Whitney, and Amber were all holding their coffee cups in the air, as if frozen in time. Amber's jaw dropped slightly. After several seconds of stunned silence from the group, Amber asked, "How did you *do* all of that so quickly?"

"I guess I realized that I can either spend my time being irritated and frustrated and overwhelmed, or I can do something about the irritation and frustration and overwhelm. I decided to do something about it,"

Cecilia said. "I was expending all sorts of energy on these things that seemed outside of my control—other people, the issues within our division, what felt like an inability to reclaim my time and calendar. But then it hit me that only I could change those things. My own little lightbulb moment," Cecilia said, with a laugh.

"Well, cheers to that!" Monique said enthusiastically. The four clinked their coffee cups and smiled. "Leadership isn't for the faint of heart," Whitney said. "Isn't that the truth," agreed Cecilia. They smiled at each other in a moment of shared understanding as they finished up the last few pieces of the raspberry scone.

Our opportunity is to create from whatever is happening around us. No matter what we are facing, no matter what we are navigating, and no matter what circumstances are arising, there is always something that we can create. It might be small, and the change we desire might be slow, but we *always* have a choice about how we show up and how we respond. As we explored earlier, we have 1,440 minutes in a 24-hour day. Every moment is a leadership moment—an opportunity to be awake and alive to what is happening around us.

There will always be many things on our mind and many things that we are concerned about. As leaders, we can continuously ask ourselves, What can I influence? What can I positively shift or change? What can I impact? What is one small shift that I can make *right now*, right here, in this moment?

By doing the deep work we have explored together, we are learning about who we are as leaders and as humans. We are looking in the mirror and getting curious about how our actions, behaviors, and thought patterns may or may not be creating the results that we desire. With this new awareness, we can continually ask ourselves, "How can I use what I'm learning to positively create from the situation that is before me?"

Applying this mindset, I have seen clients create jobs that weren't posted and that previously didn't exist and negotiate salaries for twice as much as what they thought was possible. I have watched CEOs lead their organizations through their best year in history, in the middle of a recession or a global pandemic. I have observed friends and colleagues create their ideal partnerships. When we enter into relationship with our world and continue to create from it, anything is possible.

No matter what is or isn't happening...

No matter who is or isn't involved...

No matter whether we like the situation or not...

We have a choice about how we respond to the moment that is before us. As we now know, leadership happens in the moments.

EXPLORE

MOMENTS HAPPEN TO US	WE CREATE FROM THE MOMENTS BEFORE US
We are at the mercy of the world around us—our external circumstances dictate our inner happiness and fulfillment.	We consciously create from whatever is happening around us.
We allow the current to sweep us away.	We consciously and intentionally swim with the current—and when the current runs against us, we pause to consider what it is teaching us.
It is someone else's fault.	We look for our areas of impact and responsibility.
We spend our energy being frustrated, disgruntled, or irritated with others and/or our situation.	We put our energy into creating some sort of positive shift related to the things that frustrate us.
Life happens *to* me.	Life is happening *for* me.

REFLECT

1. What does it look like to create from the moment that is before me?

2. What is one area of my work, leadership, or life in which I'd like to positively create change? What is one small step I can take toward this intention?

3. Where am I externalizing my world—blaming outside factors for my happiness or success? What could it look like to look in the mirror and consider what I can create from this situation?

4. What is one small (or large) frustration in my work or life? What is one small (or large) action that I can take to improve it?

5. What could be different if I trusted that life is happening *for me*?

CONCLUSION

AND

REFLECTIONS

Thank you for reading, and for leading. May you go forth to tackle the toughest spiritual tornados, the loneliest leadership moments, and your own versions of the Anti-Marshmallow Campaign with more confidence, clarity, and joy. May you journey from here with a few new tools in your metaphorical pack.

As you know by now, leadership happens in the moments. Becoming a leader doesn't mean that we must become someone else, but rather, that we have an opportunity to expand into all of who we are.

Our world needs you to lead. In big and small ways, in large and small moments, with others and on your own. You have everything within you to lead with compassion, consciousness, clarity, curiosity, courage, and creativity. You always have.

Here's to leadership, to walking along the ever-winding path, to accepting that it will likely be messy, and to continuing the journey anyway. Here's to taking a stand for the type of organizations that we want to work in, and the type of world that we want to live in. Here's to creating Expansive Impact in our leadership and our lives.

Thank you again for being here and for reading. You are part of the shift toward a more conscious and compassionate world. On the pages that follow, you will find additional ways to connect, to keep the conversation alive, and to put these practices into action.

With Gratitude,

Sarah

STAYING CONNECTED FROM HERE

Free Resources for Expansive Impact

If you would like to deepen your learning and application, you may enjoy the following free resources:

- EXPANSIVE IMPACT ONLINE LIBRARY: You will find a free library of reflections, resources, and templates for this book, as well as a downloadable action plan, at zingcollaborative.com/book.
- FRIDAY FAVORITES: This is a way to start your Fridays with intention and joy. It is a weekly email that offers a reflection and invitation for the week, along with recommendations on what to read, listen to, and explore further. It includes questions to incorporate into your journaling practice, or with your team. Several community members have shared that it's their favorite way to start their Fridays or their weekends—for many, over coffee or tea, during a few quiet morning moments. If you're interested in joining the conversation, you can do so by signing up via the website zingcollaborative.com.

Working Together

Through my boutique leadership development company Zing Collaborative, I am grateful to work with a select group of highly conscious, heart-centered, and intentional leaders who want to take their impact and their organizations to the next level. Current clients range from large, multinational, multibillion dollar manufacturing firms, to regional construction companies, to fully remote technology companies. The common thread among my clients is that they have invested leaders who see the long-term vision, and who believe in supporting and developing the people who are making the vision a reality.

If your team, company, or organization could benefit from the concepts in this book by working together in a more hands-on way, I would be delighted to speak with you. This work could include:

- NATURE-BASED EXPANSIVE IMPACT EXPERIENCES: highly impactful and thoughtfully curated leadership-based experiences for your team or organization, set to the backdrop of nature.
- TRAIN THE TRAINER: empowering individuals within your organization to teach and coach others how to lead more effectively in the moments, through the Six Invitations of Expansive Impact.
- EXPANSIVE IMPACT FOR ORGANIZATIONS, TEAMS, AND GROUPS: in-house experiences for your organization, team, group, or association.
- EXPANSIVE IMPACT FOR NEW, EMERGING, OR EXECUTIVE LEADERS: an in-house experience, tailored to the specific needs of your leadership group.
- SPEAKING, WORKSHOPS, AND EVENTS: bringing Expansive Impact to your conference or event in the form of an interactive keynote speech or workshop.
- WOMEN'S COACHING CIRCLES: intimate, virtual circles made up of remarkable women leaders.
- EXPANSIVE IMPACT DINNER PARTIES: a better way to gather. Deep conversation, delicious food, and surprise and delight.

GRATITUDE AND
ACKNOWLEDGMENTS

would first like to honor all who have come before. The realms of personal, professional, and leadership development are not new, and there are many great teachers, thinkers, authors, and creators who have paved the way.

There are a many specific teachers and leaders whose work has inspired mine, with a few that I'd like to thank specifically. In addition to the many great thinkers, authors, and teachers referenced throughout the book, I'd like to extend abundant gratitude to Co-Active Training Institute, CRR Global, Franklin Covey, Byron Katie, The Gottman Institute, Jon Kabat-Zinn, and Thich Nhat Hanh. Your teachings have been instrumental in shaping my perspectives. Thank you.

First, Stephen R. Covey and the Covey Institute. When I was working in the corporate world, this was the first "management book" that we were asked to read. I personally believe that *The 7 Habits of Highly Effective People* was, and is, one of the most influential personal development books ever written. Many of the concepts that have become popular, flashy, and named with catchy titles today are concepts that Covey talked about (albeit more subtly) decades ago.

Second, I would like to thank the Co-Active Training Institute, formerly known as the Coaches Training Institute. Completing the Co-Active Coach Training Program, and especially the Co-Active Leadership Program, were two of the most shaping experiences of my adult life. The spirit of Co-Active is alive within me every single day and has influenced how I show up in the world—as both a leader and a human. I think about the many things I would do differently during my early days in the corporate world, if only I would have had these remarkable tools, insights, and ways of being during that time. A special thank you to Carey and Sam, my fearless leadership leaders, for generously pouring yourselves into our program, our tribe, and into each one of us as individuals. Carey, thank you for being my first coach and such an important guide on my own leadership path. I love you to pieces.

Third, I'd like to thank Byron Katie. Byron Katie created a model called *The Work*, which you will find referenced several times throughout this book. Katie has made this work widely available for free, with countless templates, tools, and frameworks—all of which can be downloaded from her website. Her work has been modified, expanded, and built upon by many others in this space, oftentimes without credit, and she remains infinitely generous. Thank you for sharing your wisdom and your life-changing practice with all of us.

And finally, I'd like to thank the authors, creators, and thinkers in this space who have come before. We are grateful to live in a time when personal, professional, and leadership development are widely accepted topics. The coaching industry has taken off rapidly in the last decade, and many people are hungry to learn and grow. This was not the case only a few years ago, and I am infinitely grateful to those who have tirelessly worked to serve this space and the many people who benefit from these bodies of work.

Thank you. . .

To my remarkable clients, for bringing immense joy to my life and to my work. For inspiring me continuously with your brilliance and heart. For trusting me to walk alongside you on this journey.

To the Fab Four - the greatest gift that emerged from our pandemic year. Our conversations, friendship, and container are pure nourishment, and I am beyond grateful.

To Jenny, for our joyful morning trips to the ice cream shop, for our countless ASGs, and for our sacred container of friendship, authorship, and all things work and life. I am so grateful for you, and I am overjoyed that our books are siblings.

To Dana, my soul sister. Thank you for seeing me, for reflecting back things that I can't always see in myself, for our divinely guided path, and our friendship. I love you everything.

To Jake, for shared adventures big and small, for calmly and knowingly nudging me to go do a few minutes of exercise when I'm feeling agitated, for steady and grounded support, for your commitment to a shared vision, and for partnering to create a whole which is greater than the sum of its parts.

To Mom and Dad, for endless love and support for this book, for The Whale Story, and for everything in between. I love you all the way to Florida and back.

To Lindsay, for generously sharing your knowledge about all things branding and book; for being a sister from another lifetime; for modeling the way of beauty, thoughtfulness, and owning our value. Thank you for being *Lindsay In Our Pocket* for questions large and small!

To Laura, for modeling the way of fearlessness, clarity, and action and for seeing and reflecting my genius in such a helpful way.

To Jackie H. For lovingly, periodically nudging me that I need to write a book—and for modeling integrity, optimism, and the ability to use every day to the max. You are a continuous inspiration.

To Tammy, for being an early reader, for seeing and appreciating me and my work, and for the many gifts you bring to my life. I am infinitely grateful that we met.

To Ellen, for being an early reader, for contributing so much to Alchemy and our circles, and for being a bright light.

To Megan B, for our friendship, your thoughtfulness, and for our joyful and grounding conversations.

To Rebecca DH, for our friendship and wide-spanning and life-giving conversations.

To Amanda S, thank you for your friendship, for providing input on very early structural concepts for the book, and for your continued encouragement that the 999 tragedies could indeed become 999 possibilities!

To Bobbie, for working your magic from behind the lens, for your friendship, and for our shared love of early mornings, coffee, and island life.

To the incredible women in my women's circles, thank you for the containers that we create together. Our conversations and circles are pure joy, and I am so grateful for each of you.

Thank you to everyone who provided contributions in various forms, from stories and reflections; to early input on the title, subtitle, and concepts for the book; to periodic reviews; to blurbs; to encouragement along the way.

To Chariti and Darcy. Many years ago when I decided that I was going to leave my job to become a coach, I reached out to both of you. You were gracious, helpful, and generous with your time, your knowledge, and your support. You are both professionals, and models of pure classiness in the coaching space. Thank you both.

To Andrea, Scott, and my Alignment Yoga community. Our time together helped me see a bigger world beyond the corporate world that I was in at the time, and it helped me to slow down during a time when I was running at full speed. While I didn't know it at the time, this part of my journey was planting seeds for what would later become Zing Collaborative.

Andrea, thank you for creating beautiful escapes that allow inspiration to come through. Thank you for our friendship, our conversations and connection, and for our shared love of warm weather and big water.

To Jess S, thank you for being the first person I called after my family, when I decided that I wanted to start my own business.

To Lisa B, thank you for being a badass at what you do and for being with me for almost two decades now. You are truly brilliant at your craft.

To Doug S, for generously offering to talk with me when I said I wanted to write a book. Our phone call several years ago was one of the first official steps along this journey.

To our Sarahendipity pod, thank you for the joyful conversations that were paving the way for this book to later emerge.

To my first manager in the corporate world, Lyndsay. You modeled heart-centered leadership from day one, and you continue to do so today. I'm so grateful for the way that our paths have come full-circle.

To JB, thank you for seeing my potential as a coach and a leader, for being a caring advocate, and for pushing me to step outside my comfort zone. Much of the work from this chapter of my career helped to spark my interest in coaching others, which ultimately led me toward today. Thank you.

To my staff management executive gals, thank you for our endless hours together in conference rooms. While this was an intensely difficult period, our moments of laughter and our casual group therapy sessions were a lifeline.

To Devin, thank you for being my partner in crime and for your friendship during the hardest chapter of my professional career.

To my Gundersen team, both internal and external. Thank you for being a dream team. I loved working with you, and our time together was a professional highlight.

To JZ, thank you for being one of the most incredible leaders who I've ever had the privilege of working with. You continue to model the way for inspirational leadership.

To the team members I had the privilege of managing in the corporate world, thank you for showing up, for inspiring me, and for helping me find the path that I'm on today.

To my Peacocks, I am so grateful for our shared journey together.

To my GSD BOD, thank you for our inspiring, supportive, joyful, and uplifting conversations over the years.

To Amanda B, thank you for your friendship, for our connection from afar, for being a Friday Favorites superfan, and for being an inspiration related to motherhood, creativity, and life. I am so glad we were able to share bug spray on that fateful day back in CR.

To Laura S, for providing loving support as I worked on this book.

To JP, for helping to make me a more compassionate, understanding, and empathetic human being.

To Afton and Gwen, for being such bright lights in my life. I love you to pieces. Please keep shining brightly.

To Mara, for your ability to uncover the essence and then create it.

To Kym and Mark, for your love and support.

To Jess, for our friendship and our alchemy.

To Ron, for risking it all in service of my own growth in the front of the room.

To Mrs. A, for helping to bring my very first 'published work' forth to the young author's fair.

To Markus, for seeing the possibility within your organization and for taking a stand for leadership. I'm so grateful that our paths crossed on that fateful day.

To NS, MK, and EZ, for being some of my earliest official coaching clients and for trusting me to walk beside you on your path. Thank you.

To the coaches I've had the pleasure of working with, thank you.

To Vic, for your coaching and now for your friendship and our ongoing conversations.

To Lee, for printing out countless copies of this in-progress manuscript and for being one of my favorite humans.

To my aunt CL, for our postcards, conversations, and our connection.

To my cousin D, for our emails, our conversations, and for our continuous reflections on life, work, travel, food, pups, and all the good stuff. Our conversations are a joy.

To Kristin, for helping to bring the words of this book to life through your wisdom and heart via editing. I am so grateful that you were my first editor.

To Nina, Hobbs, Nicole, Caitlin, Ben, Gregg, and the Amplify team, for helping to bring this book forth in the world.

To everyone who contributed stories, perspectives, insights, and quotes for this book. Your words and wisdom are gifts.

And to everyone who I'm lucky enough to call a client, colleague, or friend, thank you for enriching my life. I am deeply grateful.

ENDNOTES

INTRODUCTION

1   Less than 30 percent of managers strongly agree that someone at work encourages their development. This Gallup statistic comes from *It's the Manager* by Jim Clifton and Jim Harter.

2   1% for the Planet believes that because companies profit from resources they take from the earth, they should protect those resources. Members donate 1 percent of all sales back to the environment by supporting a diverse group of approved environmental organizations. It was founded by Yvon Chouinard of Patagonia and Craig Mathews of Blue Ribbon Flies in 2002.

SECTION ONE

1   For additional ways to reclaim a few moments during the day, you can visit www.zingcollaborative.com/book. Here, you'll find an online resource library to supplement the book.

2   For more, you may enjoy reading "How Leaders Inspire: Cracking the Code," published by Bain & Company.

3   There are hundreds of studies reflecting the impact of a regular gratitude practice. A few to check out as a starting point: "Giving Thanks Can Make You Happier" from *Harvard Health Publishing*, "How Gratitude Changes You and Your Brain" from *Berkeley* and "The 7 Scientifically Proven Benefits of Gratitude" via *Psychology Today*.

4   For more, consider visiting the Centre for Justice and Reconciliation.

5   *Self-Compassion Step by Step: The Proven Power of Being Kind to Yourself* by Kristin Neff.

6   Per Kristin Neff's research, this means taking a balanced approach to our negative emotions so that feelings are neither suppressed nor exaggerated. It invites us to hold our thoughts and emotions into a greater context and larger perspective, rather than being overidentified with thoughts and feelings.

7   For more, check out Maria Shriver and Elizabeth Lesser's interview in which they discuss this topic, as well as Tim Ferriss and Elizabeth Lesser's podcast episode on *The Tim Ferriss Show*.

8   This idea comes from Friedrich Nietzsche.

9   Holding neutral means practicing acknowledging our current reality, without rushing to place a judgment on it. This could mean saying "it is" rather than "it is good" or "it is bad."

SECTION TWO

1   For more, you may enjoy checking out *The Work* by Byron Katie.

2   In this case, "moving on" could mean moving forward and putting the issue behind us, exploring new possibilities, or making a bigger change such as transferring to a new team or looking for a new job.

3   You will find a template for these activities at www.zingcollaborative.com/book.

4   Here, I'd like to thank one of my teachers, Sam House, for offering the language of "low and to the left." Thank you, Sam, for this and for your many gifts on my own leadership journey.

5   The term impostor syndrome can be traced to a 1978 article by the American psychologists Pauline Clance and Suzanne Imes, "The Imposter Phenomenon in High Achieving Women: Dynamics and Therapeutic Intervention." Originally called impostor phenomenon, impostor syndrome, as it's now usually called, is commonly understood as a false and sometimes crippling belief that one's successes are the product of luck or fraud rather than skill.

6   *When Things Fall Apart* by Pema Chodron is a beautiful book that I highly recommend. It is particularly helpful if you are gripping tightly to something that you might need to let go of; if you are going through a hard period; or if you are craving a reminder that whatever is happening right now is part of the path.

7   For more on this concept, you may enjoy reading the book *Flow: The Psychology of Optimal Experience* by Mihaly Csikszentmihalyi.

8   Conscientiousness is the personality trait of a person who shows an awareness of the impact that their own behavior has on those around them. The *Big Five* is a grouping, for personality traits, developed from the 1980s onward in psychological trait theory.

9   For a downloadable worksheet for this exercise, please visit www.zingcollaborative.com/book.

10   The "Parable of the Fisherman" is said to have originated in Brazil. It involves a fisherman, living a beautiful and quiet life, who is pressured by a businessman to do *more*—catch and sell more fish, make more money, and achieve more success, only to then retire so that he can do what he's already doing: spend his days fishing and his evenings with his family, enjoying the thing he loves, living a beautiful and quiet life. If ever you find yourself in a spiral of chasing external success, I highly recommend reading or re-reading this parable.

SECTION THREE

1   This quote is most commonly attributed to Isaac Asimov. That said, there is some debate over the original source, who some say is Alan Alda, an actor and comedian who played Hawkeye Pierce in *M*A*S*H*.

2   The Four Horsemen of the Apocalypse is a metaphor depicting the end of times in the New Testament, describing conquest, war, hunger, and death, respectively. The Gottman Institute uses this metaphor to describe communication styles that, according to their research, can predict the end of a relationship. My observation is that these behaviors present not only in personal relationships, but within teams and organizations as well.

3   For additional reading, you may enjoy *The Four Agreements* by Don Miguel Ruiz.

4   Here, I'd like to thank my friend Chariti for helping me combine these questions in a way that not only explores current assumptions, but also possibilities without them.

5   For more on this concept, you may enjoy reading the article "Employees Who Feel Love Perform Better" by Sigal Barsade and Olivia A. O'Neill in *Harvard Business Review*. It is based on a study called "What's Love Got to Do with It?"

6   Here, we use the word "hooked" to represent the idea of being psychologically addicted to someone or something. This sometimes happens with other people; with issues or topics; or with external events. If we highly triggered or are obsessively dwelling on someone or something, it is a clue that we might be hooked.

7   Tiny Boxes on the Calendar is the name I've given to the scenario in which my calendar is filled with commitments, without ample time to focus on big picture thinking, strategy, or deep work. My continuous practice is to work toward a balance of time-related commitments, alongside white space for thinking and creating.

8   Per Kahn, psychological safety is defined as "being able to show and employ one's self without fear of negative consequences of self-image, status, or career."

9   During one of the most challenging periods of my professional career, I would reconnect to this quote nearly every day. A loved one in my life would remind me of this quote during phone calls. It helped me to show up with strength, even in the most difficult circumstances.

10   Thank you to my friend, Jenny H, for teaching me this mind-blowing nugget about the lesser-known fourth response.

11   You'll find more in the article "Gwyneth Paltrow Gets Real about Past Relationships, Her Place in the #MeToo Movement, and Why She Quit Acting for Good" by Josh Duboff, *Harper's Bazaar*.

12   "How to Ask Your Mentors for Help" by Derek Sivers. You can find this excellent post on Derek's blog, via this link: https://sive.rs/ment.

13   For a list of tips from other leaders on how to deal with saboteurs, gremlins, and thinking traps, please visit www.zingcollaborative.com/book.

14   The Triple Bottom Line includes People, Profit, and Planet. It suggests that organizations should commit to measuring their social and environmental impact, in addition to their financial performance.

15   I use this decision filter not only for sponsorships, but also for how and where I donate money and time each year. Having a decision filter based on values can make hard decisions easier.

16   Thank you to CTI, CRR Global, and Priya Parker for the excellent work you are doing related to these concepts. Thank you to CTI for inspiring the language of Stake.

17   If you find yourself with a complaining team member or colleague in your office, before you immediately take on the weight of their complaints and move toward solutioning, it can be helpful to pause and ask, "Would you like me to do something with this information, or do you just need to vent?" I observe many managers taking on team members' problems to *solve,* when in reality the team member just wanted to *vent.* Clarifying up front can be helpful.

18   Making Cheesecake is an expression that two of my clients came up with, as an alternative to walking on eggshells. As someone who loves dessert, I am a big fan of this reframe!

19   For a hilarious article examining the difference between the two, I highly recommend "Vacation or Trip? A Helpful Guide for Parents," by M. Blazoned, on *HuffPost*.

20   For a list of additional questions we can use to clarify expectations, please visit www.zingcollaborative.com/book.

SECTION FOUR

1   *The Confidence Gap* and *The Confidence Code* are both written by Katty Kay and Claire Shipman and address the question of competence versus confidence, with specific focus on how this question applies to women.

2   The Dunning–Kruger effect is a hypothetical cognitive bias stating that people with low ability at a task overestimate their own ability, and that people with high ability at a task underestimate their own ability. It was named after social psychologists David Dunning and Justin Kruger.

3   This research comes from the study called "Managers Believe They Motivate Employees More Than They Actually Do," which was published via the *Norwegian Job Behavior Report* in 2019.

4   "The Parable of the Trapeze" by Danaan Parry is an article that explores the idea of turning fear of transformation into transformation of fear.

5   For more, you may enjoy checking out the book *Deep Listening* by Pauline Oliveros.

6   *The Gift of Fear* by Gavin DeBecker is a great book, especially if you tend to override your intuition with your logical mind.

7   Gratitude to the many great thinkers who have tackled the art of asking better questions over the years. Also, during workshops, many times people ask about the absence of *why* questions. *Why* questions certainly have a place. That said, most of us are better at asking *why* questions than at asking *what* or *how* questions, so this is an opportunity to aim low and left, to expand our leadership capacity. Additionally, *why* questions often take us to the past to find root cause (which can be helpful, depending on the situation), where *what* or *how* questions take us to a place of possibility. Depending on the framing, *why* questions can also unintentionally put others on the defensive.

8   Rebecca learned about this question from one of her students, who said that it came from pre-Socratic philosopher Meno. That said, the original source is somewhat (or totally) unknown!

9   You will find a full list of curiosity-based questions to try in different types of situations at www.zingcollaborative.com/book.

10 *The One Minute Manager Meets the Monkey* by Ken Blanchard is a helpful (and brief) book for anyone who has trouble delegating. It offers a simple four-step framework that involves describing the monkey, assigning the monkey, ensuring the monkey, and checking on the monkey.

11 To access a coaching cheat sheet for managers and leaders, please visit www.zingcollaborative.com/book.

12 You will find a full list of questions to try, as well as a cheat sheet to use in coaching conversations with team members at www.zingcollaborative.com/book.

13 *The Coaching Habit* by Michael Bungay Stanier is a great little book for flexing our coaching muscles. It is a quick and punchy read.

14 Some of the organizations have renamed their Human Resource divisions, choosing alternate names such as People Operations, Employee Experience, Talent Management, or Employee Success.

SECTION FIVE

1 For more on this concept, you may enjoy checking out the fields of biophilia and biomimicry.

2 For an excellent book on this topic, I highly recommend *Why Talking Is Not Enough* by Susan Page. It pushes against the common wisdom that all problems in relationships should be solved through dialogue, and instead suggests transforming our relationships into spiritual partnerships through eight loving actions. While the book was written for romantic relationships, many of the principles can be applied in friendships and at work.

3 Per Kahn, Psychological safety is defined as "being able to show and employ one's self without fear of negative consequences of self-image, status, or career."

4 This comes from "The Five Keys to a Successful Google Team" by Julia Rozovsky, an Analyst for Google People Operations.

5   Informed and inspired by the world's longest-lived cultures, the mission of the Blue Zones is to empower everyone, everywhere to live longer, better. The Blue Zones was founded by author and adventurer Dan Buettner, who traveled around the world to learn the secrets of the world's longest-living people.

6   *It's the Manager* by Jim Clifton and Jim Harter is a book that summarizes some of Gallup's research related to teams and managers.

7   Here, it is important to note that this method of feedback delivery does not require us to shut off our critical thinking skills, or our intuition about what might be going on. Rather, it is another opportunity to aim low and left, so that we can land closer to the bull's-eye of specific, actionable, and useful feedback.

8   During the editing process, it was suggested by one of my beloved editors that some managers use the sandwich method with great success and that I should not write off the sandwich method as an effective method of sharing feedback. While I very much appreciate this perspective, having worked with thousands of leaders and employees over the course of multiple decades, I have not yet found a single person who has said, "I love when my manager uses the sandwich method!" So, if you use the sandwich method, please feel free to keep both of these perspectives in mind.

9   "Picking someone's brain" is commonly defined as gathering information or ideas from someone else's brain to use for our own purposes. As a side note, it is one of my least favorite phrases!

10 For more, you may enjoy "The Importance of Mourning Losses (Even When They Seem Small)," NPR.

11 If you find yourself the recipient of a surprising, shocking, or even traumatic or violent outburst after telling the truth with heart, I recommend researching the topic of narcissistic rage. It is possible that you have just experienced it firsthand. For more, feel free to search for his topic at zingcollaborative. com/blog.

12 For example, due to the consumption of drugs or alcohol.

13 *Thanks for the Feedback* by Shelia Heen and Douglas Stone is a well-researched, in-depth read on the topic of feedback.

SECTION SIX

1   A system is any combination of multiple people, for example: a partnership, a team, a neighborhood, a company, or a nonprofit board.

2   To download a template for this exercise, please visit www.zingcollaborative. com/book.

3   A pro/pro or a con/con list involves rethinking the traditional pro/con list to think through the positives about all options, and the negatives about all options. In other words, it is a tactical tool to help uncover more expansive options and possible Third Paths.

INDEX